Watch Your Words

Watch Your Words

A Writing and Editing Handbook for the Multimedia Age

FOURTH EDITION

Marda Dunsky

ROWMAN & LITTLEFIELD
Lanham • Boulder • New York • London

Published by Rowman & Littlefield
A wholly owned subsidiary of The Rowman & Littlefield Publishing Group, Inc.
4501 Forbes Boulevard, Suite 200, Lanham, Maryland 20706
www.rowman.com

Unit A, Whitacre Mews, 26-34 Stannary Street, London SE11 4AB, United Kingdom

British Library Cataloguing in Publication Information Available

Library of Congress Cataloging-in-Publication Data

Dunsky, Marda.
   Watch your words : a writing and editing handbook for the multimedia age / Marda
   Dunsky. — Fourth edition.
      pages cm
   Includes index.
   ISBN 978-1-4422-5342-1 (cloth : alk. paper) — ISBN 978-1-4422-5343-8 (pbk. : alk. paper) —
   ISBN 978-1-4422-5344-5 (electronic) 1. Journalism—Style manuals. I. Title.
   PN4783.D86 2015
   808.06'607—dc23

                                                                              2015012728

Printed in the United States of America

Contents

Getting Text Right

I recently ran into a journalist who took a language-skills seminar I had given more than a decade ago at a major newspaper. A veteran of broadcast, online and print media, he not only remembered but also thanked me for the drills I'd put him through.

"In an age when radio, TV and newspaper compete against one another on the Internet, journalists don't have to choose between working in print, on air or on the Web," he said. "They need to do it all: Radio and TV people have to know how to write, and newspaper people have to know how to talk."

In this era of multimedia journalism, text has more company than ever before. Journalists use audio, video, photography and other interactive graphics to bring immediacy, impact and relatability to their work. Journalism instruction reflects these changes, often with less time devoted to basic writing and editing skills.

However, text remains a powerful medium to convey simple and complex ideas that can't always be told visually — and the written word is often part of multimedia storytelling. Using language well is an important skill for journalists across platforms. The cleaner and clearer the text, the more effective the result.

Watch Your Words, now in its fourth edition, is distinguished from other language-skills reference works by its brevity. *WYW* is an accessible handbook for mastering a baseline knowledge of punctuation, grammar, usage and Associated Press style. It can be used with or independent of a course syllabus and online language-skills programs.

New in this edition is a quality-control guide to writing and editing that covers accuracy and fact-checking; brevity and tightening; clarity; use of quotations and attribution; and basic editing principles. This edition also incorporates current AP style and continues to feature language-skills self-tests with answer keys as well as sections on spelling and copy-editing symbols.

In its presentation of language skills, *Watch Your Words* addresses objective rules (when to choose *who* over *whom*, for example) as well as subjective language-use guidelines. It's important to remember, though, that language is flexible. Other reference works contain rules and guidelines that vary from those in *WYW* — and applications may also vary.

Watch Your Words reflects choices made for the sake of journalistic simplicity, logic and consistency (mainly with AP). It provides a brief but solid overview of basic language skills and writing and editing techniques that holds up across platforms and over time.

Write and edit well!
Marda Dunsky

Punctuation

The objective of correct punctuation is **clarity**.

The right punctuation is to good writing what artful seasoning is to well-prepared food. Used properly, those commas, semicolons and dashes not only enhance pacing and tone but also render intended meanings clear.

Consider the following, of unknown authorship:

■ The Importance of Proper Punctuation

Gloria wrote the same letter to John on two different days using the same words, changing only the punctuation. Which was John happier to receive?

Dear John:

I want a man who knows what love is all about. You are generous, kind, thoughtful. People who are not like you admit to being useless and inferior. You have ruined me for other men. I yearn for you. I have no feelings whatsoever when we're apart. I can be forever happy — will you let me be yours?

Gloria

◆ ◆ ◆

Dear John:

I want a man who knows what love is. All about you are generous, kind, thoughtful people, who are not like you. Admit to being useless and inferior.

You have ruined me. For other men, I yearn. For you, I have no feelings whatsoever. When we're apart, I can be forever happy. Will you let me be?

Yours,
Gloria

Rules and Guidelines

Apostrophes

generally are used for simple possessives: *The book is Mary's.*

singular *vs.*
plural possessive

They are also used for *quasi-possessives*, which show possession in a figurative rather than a literal sense. Positioning of the apostrophe for possessives and quasi-possessives depends on whether the sense is singular (*'s*) or plural (*s'*).

> Rebecca earned a week's pay for a day's work.
>
> Miguel earned two weeks' pay for two days' work.

descriptive *vs.*
possessive

Adjectives that are **descriptive** rather than possessive do not take apostrophes. This is the case when the words *by* or *for* are implicit in the meaning.

> The teachers strike is in its third week.
> *(the strike by teachers)*
>
> The freelancer bought a writers guide.
> *(a guide for writers)*

its *vs.* **it's**

A very common (and embarrassing) error is using **its** when **it's** is called for or vice versa. *Its* is possessive; *it's* is a contraction that stands for *it is* (not *it has* or *it was*).

> Put everything in its place.
>
> It's the thought that counts.

years:
omitted digits

Use an apostrophe to indicate omitted digits that would denote a century. Don't use an apostrophe when indicating a decade using all four digits.

> Russell was born in the mid-'50s.
>
> The 1960s was a turbulent decade.

Brackets

are used to insert words that the speaker did not say into direct quotes for clarity. This should be done sparingly and judiciously. (*See* **Parentheses**.)

> "This is the most difficult I have run," the mayor said.
>
> "This is the most difficult [election campaign] I have run," the mayor said.

Colons have three primary functions:

- to introduce **a concept or an idea**

> Here's what I think: Better days are sure to come.

Note the capital "B" in *Better*. The first word after a colon is capitalized when it introduces a thought that can stand on its own as a complete sentence.

- to introduce **a list**

> The basket was filled with exotic fruit: mangoes, kiwis and pomegranates.

Note that *mangoes* is not capitalized because the list it introduces cannot stand on its own as a complete sentence.

- to set off **attribution** at the beginning of a **multisentence quote**

> The coach said: "The loyalty of the student body means a lot to me. I will finish my contract and not entertain offers from other schools."

Commas are used to separate or set off the following:

simple series

A series (at least three elements) can consist of single words, phrases or clauses. (A clause requires a verb; a phrase does not.) In a simple series, a comma is not used before the *and* preceding the final element.

> The colors of the French flag are blue, white and red.
>
> Sam did the laundry, cleaned the house and cooked dinner.

simple-series exception

The exception to the no-serial-comma rule occurs when the final element of the series contains the conjunction *and*. In this case insert a comma after the second-to-last element and before the *and* that immediately follows it.

> The appetizers included carrot sticks, olives, and cheese and crackers.

Change the order of the series, and the no-serial-comma rule applies:

> The appetizers included cheese and crackers, carrot sticks and olives.

independent clauses, same subject

Separate independent clauses that have the same subject (including *you* understood) with a comma (or two).

> Feed a cold, starve a fever.
>
> We saw it, we wanted it, we bought it.

long intro clauses, phrases

✔ **Long** introductory clauses and phrases of **more than three words** are set off with commas for pacing.

🚫 **Short** introductory clauses and phrases of **three words or fewer** generally don't require commas.

> When Jane left her husband of 20 years, she felt sad.
>
> When Jane left she felt sad.
>
> In 2012 Jane left her husband of 20 years.

The **exception** is made for the sake of clarity. Use a comma when its absence would make the sentence unclear or result in a sentence fragment.

> Ever since, I've had a craving for anchovies.

coordinate (equal) **adjectives**

Coordinate adjectives have equal weight.

✔ **They can be transposed logically and are separated by commas.**

> Jana inherited a colorful, old carpet.
>
> Jana inherited an old, colorful carpet.

noncoordinate adjectives

Noncoordinate adjectives do not have equal weight.

🚫 **They cannot be transposed logically and are not separated by commas.**

> Jana inherited a colorful Oriental carpet.

Conjunction Junction:
Comma Rules for *and*, *but* and *or*

and   ⊘   1.   If **no subject** follows *and*, then no comma precedes it.

> I finished studying and then went to a movie.

⊘   2.   If the clauses joined by *and* have the **same subject**, and they are **closely related** in meaning (the second being a logical result of the first), then don't use a comma before *and*.

> I finished reading the book and then I called my sister to talk about it.

✔   3.   If the clauses joined by *and* have the **same subject**, but they are **not closely related** in meaning, then use a comma before *and*.

> I finished reading the book, and then I called my sister.

✔   4.   If the clauses joined by *and* have **different subjects,** then use a comma before *and* whether or not the clauses are closely related.

> I wrote the paper, and my roommate edited it.

but   ✔   1.   Use a comma before *but* if a **subject** (same or different) **is stated** after it.

> Nader ran for president, but I did not vote for him.
> Nader ran for president, but he did not win.

⊘   2.   Don't use a comma before *but* if **no subject is stated** after it.

> Nader ran for president but did not win.

or   ✔   1.   Use a comma before *or* when the **second subject is different**.

> Jack is the best on the team, or Notre Dame wouldn't have given him a scholarship.

⊘   2.   Don't use a comma before *or* when the **subjects** before and after it **are the same**.

> Jack is the best on the team or he thinks he is.

Nonessential *vs.* Essential: *That vs.* **Which**

nonessential elements

Nonessential elements can be removed from the sentence, and its meaning will remain clear.

> Roger gave his only sister, Emily, a flute.

If Roger has only one sister, her name is not essential to understanding the meaning of the sentence.

✔ **Nonessential (nonrestrictive) elements are set off with commas.**

nonessential: *which*

Most, but not all, phrases and clauses that start with *which* are nonessential and are set off with commas.

> The concert, which is the last of the tour, is sold out.

The essence of this sentence is that the concert is sold out. The fact that it is the last of the tour is supplementary information.

essential elements

Essential elements cannot be removed from the sentence if its meaning is to remain clear.

> The comedy "Liar Liar" is playing downtown.

Presumably many comedies are playing downtown — thus the title of the film is essential to the meaning of the sentence.

🚫 **Essential (restrictive) elements are not set off with commas.**

essential: *that*

Most, but not all, phrases and clauses that start with *that* are essential and are not set off with commas.

> The concert that is the last of the tour is sold out.

This sentence implies that there is more than one concert. Thus the concert referred to here is distinguished from others by saying it is the last of the tour. This information is essential to the meaning of the sentence.

state names and years

State names and years are set off with commas when paired with their respective municipal entities and full dates. City and country pairings are punctuated the same way. Spell out state names in the body of a story.

> The woman from Oshkosh, Wisconsin, bought the winning lottery ticket on Nov. 22, 2005, at her neighborhood drugstore.
>
> The workers at the plant in Lyon, France, went on strike.

ages, residence

Ages and phrases denoting residence (numbered street address, city, state), with or without *of*, are set off with commas.

> Samantha Smith, 34, of Evanston, was elected to the council.
>
> Brenda Starr, of 44 Writewell Road, won a Pulitzer Prize.

elements of direct address

Elements of direct address are set off with commas, even when they appear in sentences that are not direct quotes. These elements include interjections (e.g., *yes, no, oh, well*), names and titles.

> Yes, I'm the one, officer. Oh, well, you'll just have to arrest me.
>
> You know, Jane, that's a great idea!

attribution

At the beginning of a sentence, set off attribution with a comma after the verb.

> Malika said, "I'm going to the store because we're out of milk."

In the middle of a sentence, set off attribution with two commas before the subject (inside the quote mark if a direct quote) and after the verb.

> "I'm going to the store," Malika said, "because we're out of milk."
>
> Malika was going to the store, she said, because we ran out of milk.

At the end of a sentence, set off attribution with a comma inside the quote mark and before the subject.

> "I'm going to the store because we're out of milk," Malika said.

Dashes

are used for a greater emphatic pause than semicolons or separate sentences would impart. But use them *sparingly*. Insert a space before and after dashes.

> I appreciate your help — you're the best friend I have.

Ellipses

are used to show that words, phrases or entire sentences have been omitted from a quote. Like bracketed words added to quotes for clarity, ellipses should be used *sparingly* so as not to distort meaning or context or raise questions about what has been deleted. Insert a space before and after ellipses.

> "I cannot say how touched I am by this generous show of support by my very dedicated and loyal and understanding campaign workers and constituents," the mayor said.
>
> "I cannot say how touched I am by this generous show of support by my … campaign workers and constituents," the mayor said.

Exclamation Points

are used to indicate emphasis and / or emotion, often in direct quotations. But use them *sparingly*.

> "This is the last straw!" he shouted.

Hyphens

are used to join related words to each other and prefixes to their root words.

ages

Hyphenate ages when they are used as compound adjectives but not as predicate adjectives.

> Michael has a 2-year-old son.
>
> Michael's son is 2 years old.

compound adjectives

The hyphen is placed between the adjectives, *not* between the compound adjective and the noun it modifies or describes.

> The Tribune embarked on a five-year plan to create a two-floor newsroom.

-ly

🚫 Don't hyphenate compound adjectives beginning with words that end in *-ly*.

> I got this on deep background from a highly placed source.

one word or two?

Hyphenate compound adjectives. Use two words for a noun modified by a single adjective or for adverbs.

> The company has no long-term strategy.
>
> The company is developing a strategy for the long term.
>
> He was a one-time wrestling champion.
>
> He wrestled the champion one time.
>
> Janet has a part-time job.
>
> Janet works part time.

prefixes

Consult the stylebook for individual entries. Some general rules:

✔ Hyphenate prefixes ending in the same vowel as the beginning of the root word (exceptions: *cooperate, coordinate*).

> Dr. Marcy Freud is considered to be among Chicago's pre-eminent psychiatrists.

✔ Hyphenate prefixes when the root word begins with a capital letter or number.

> Globalization is a phenomenon of the post-Cold War era.
>
> U.S. troop escalation in Vietnam started in the mid-'60s.

🚫 Don't hyphenate prefixes whose root words begin with a consonant.

> The board approved the multimillion-dollar contract.

suspensive hyphenation

Suspensive hyphenation eliminates the need to repeat an element of the compound adjective. The hyphen is suspended at the end of the first adjective or at the beginning of the second, with a space before or after *and*.

> The critic called the exhibit "a collection of second- and third-rate kitsch."
>
> WMAQ is an NBC-owned and -operated station.

well-

Hyphenate compound adjectives beginning with *well*.

> Raja is not only well-dressed, but he is also well-read.

Parentheses are used to insert words into text that is not a direct quote for clarity. (*See* **Brackets**.)

> One of the most-watched television shows (in the U.S.) is "Grey's Anatomy."

Quotation Marks have specific rules for placement of accompanying punctuation.

periods, commas Periods and commas **always** go **inside** quotation marks, whether the quoted material is a composition title, a partial quote or a full quote.

> Mary never misses an episode of "Grey's Anatomy."
>
> "I can't go with you," Mary said, "because I want to watch TV."

question marks Question marks are placed **inside** quotation marks when the quoted material is itself a question. Question marks go **outside** quotation marks when the quoted material is not a question.

> "Are you going with me?" I asked Rashid.
>
> Is this a "one-time offer"?

single quotes Use single quotes for composition titles or any other quoted material within direct quotations.

> "I can't go with you," Mary said. "I want to watch 'Grey's Anatomy.'"

Semicolons are used for two main purposes:

- to separate **independent clauses** with **different subjects** in the same sentence

> The House passed the bill; the Senate rejected it.

- to separate **elements in a complex series** that imparts information pairings, such as names and hometowns

> The conference was attended by Roger Jones, Springfield, Illinois; Joan Howard, Buffalo, New York; Howard Worthington, Little Rock, Arkansas; and Worthington Rogers, Bloomington, Indiana.

Note that the semicolon is used before *and* in a complex series.

PUNCTUATION SELF-TEST

Punctuate the following sentences correctly by inserting or deleting marks as needed. *Do not rewrite.* Some sentences are correct as is. *Key on p. 75.*

1. Professor Nelson began the lecture and passed out a quiz.

2. Professor Nelson began the lecture, but did not call on me.

3. Professor Nelson gave a long lecture but he did not use any notes.

4. Professor Nelson began the lecture and he immediately captured our attention.

5. My grandfather was reelected to a fifth term as the mayor of Hometown, Ill. on April 1, 2010 in a landslide victory.

6. They met; they dated; they broke up.

7. Here today, gone tomorrow.

8. She is survived by a sister, Rachel.

9. He is survived by his wife, Rhonda; two sons, Jules and Jim, and a grandchild, George.

10. I love epic films, especially the Oscar-winning best picture, "Titanic".

11. It was unbelievable the Wildcats pulled off another last-minute victory.

12. "When will the new budget be ready"? the alderman asked the mayor.

13. "This budget will never be passed" the alderman said. "Can you revise it?"

14. "Now this," the alderman said is a much more realistic budget."

15. The mayor called his finance officer "brilliant".

16. The mayor said "Listen colleagues, we've got to work together."

17. This year, the Board of Education averted a teachers' strike.

18. June chose white, pink, and yellow roses for her bridal bouquet.

19. Jerry served salad, garlic bread and spaghetti and meatballs for dinner.

20. He saw the car, he wanted the car, and he bought the car.

21. I like anchovy pizza, most of my friends cannot stand it.

22. My old two-story house is expensive to heat.

23. The parka was filled with soft goose down.

24. Observing the passengers on the train, she said gave her an idea for a short story.

25. Because Robert snores his wife can't get any sleep.

26. Because his snoring keeps her awake Robert and his wife sleep in separate rooms.

27. My car, which was well maintained lasted 10 years.

28. People, who live in glass houses, buy a lot of Windex.

29. The president has a five year plan for health-care reform.

30. The 26-year old man was the youngest CEO in the industry.

31. When it came to discipline, the coach treated his first and second string players alike.

32. Modernizing the stadium is a multi-million dollar project.

33. Jamila likes taking long walks. But, she likes them less in cold weather.

34. Bill gave his best friend Al some tips on fundraising.

35. Lucy gave her friend Ethel a headache.

36. The dean said "This is the best freshman class we have had in a long time. They did especially well in editing."

37. The bigamist's wife Jan was upset with her husband's other wife Suzie and Suzie's only brother Tim.

38. After the lumberjack sawed his last log cabin fever overcame him.

Grammar

You don't have to be an oracle to get grammar right. Understanding the mechanics of the language enables you to distinguish the grammatically correct from the colloquial — and to make the right choice every time.

Basic Terms and Concepts

Parts of Speech

noun denotes a person, place or thing (*student, library, book*)

> *verbal noun/gerund* a verbal form that ends in *-ing* and functions as a noun (***Skating** is fun.*)

pronoun used in place of a noun (*Lily/**she**; the class/**it**; the students/**they***)

verb denotes an action or state of being (*kick, become*)

> *infinitive* the unconjugated form of a verb, beginning with *to* (*to kick, to become*)

> *imperative* the command form of a verb; unstated subject is *you* understood (***Throw** the ball.*)

> *transitive* action verb; takes direct object (*I **gave** you the **book**.*)

> *intransitive* denotes a state of being, feeling or emotion; does not take direct object (*I **am** hungry. I **feel** tired.*)

article precedes a noun to denote indefiniteness (***a** book, **an** apple*) or definiteness (***the** chair*)

preposition a connector joining a noun or pronoun to another word, showing relationship (*I am **in** the room.*)

conjunction a connector joining words, clauses and/or phrases in a sentence (e.g., *and, but, or*)

adjective modifies or describes a noun or pronoun (***wonderful** idea, **huge** problem*)

adverb modifies or describes a verb, adjective or other adverb, often ending in *-ly* (***wonderfully** original idea*)

interjection expresses, among other things, emotion, exclamation or surprise (e.g., *ah, oh, well, wow*)

Grammatical Functions

subject
does something, has something done to it or is described
(*The **ship** sinks. / The **ship** was sunk by a torpedo. /
The **ship** is no longer seaworthy.*)

predicate
the verb in a clause (simple) or the verb and its adjectives and
objects (complete)
(*Birds **fly**. / Birds **fly south in the winter**.*)

direct object
receives the action of the <u>verb</u>
(*Jack and Jill <u>fetched</u> **a pail of water**.*)

indirect object
receives the <u>direct object</u>
(*I gave the <u>keys</u> to **you**.*)

object of preposition
the noun or pronoun in a <u>prepositional</u> phrase
(*Such is the way <u>of</u> the **world**.*)

predicate nominative
a noun or pronoun that renames the subject when the two
are joined by an <u>intransitive (linking) verb</u>
(*Superman <u>is</u> **my hero**.*)

predicate adjective
an adjective that describes the subject when the two are
joined by an <u>intransitive (linking) verb</u>
(*Superman <u>is</u> **amazing**.*)

Cases
(pronouns)

nominative case*
denotes the actor:
*I, you, he, she, it,
we, they, who, whoever*

objective case
denotes the person or thing acted upon:
*me, you, him, her, it,
us, them, whom, whomever*

possessive case
denotes the possessor:
*my (mine), your (yours), his, her (hers), its,
our (ours), their (theirs), whose*

---

* *Also known as subjective.*

GRAMMAR TERMS AND CONCEPTS EXERCISE

Key on p. 77.

I.   **Identify the parts of speech** *for each word* **in the sentences below.**
      Use the abbreviations indicated in parentheses for these choices:

      noun (**N**)   article (**art**)   adjective (**adj**)
      pronoun (**pro**)   preposition (**prep**)   adverb (**adv**)
      verb/infinitive verb (**V/inf V**)   conjunction (**conj**)   interjection (**int**)

      1. John threw the book across the room, and they gasped.

      2. Foreign languages are easy to learn when one is young.

      3. Yes, to live in France is my wildest dream.

      4. Ellie is the one who gave me the gift.

II.   **Find the grammatical functions** *of the italicized words* **in the sentences below.**
      Use the abbreviations indicated in parentheses for these choices:

      subject (**S**)   direct object (**DO**)   predicate nominative (**PN**)
      predicate (**P**)   indirect object (**IO**)   predicate adjective (**PA**)
                            object of preposition (**OP**)

      1. *John threw* the *book* across the *room,* and *they gasped.*

      2. Foreign *languages are easy* to learn when *one is young.*

      3. Yes, *to live* in France *is* my wildest *dream.*

      4. *Ellie is* the *one who gave me* the *gift.*

III. **Decline these personal pronouns according to case:**

      nominative   I   you   he   she   it   we   they   who/whoever
      objective
      possessive

Mapping *Who* vs. *Whom*

Relying on what sounds right doesn't always lead you to the right choice. If you know what grammatical function *who* or *whom* serves in a sentence, then making the correct choice is easy. Refer to the chart below:

pronoun	case	use as
WHO/ever (I, you, he, she, it, we, they)	NOMINATIVE (*also*: subjective)	subject (**S**) predicate nominative (**PN**)
WHOM/ever (me, you, him, her, it, us, them)	OBJECTIVE	direct object (**DO**) indirect object (**IO**) object of preposition (**OP**) subject of infinitive verb★

★ **The subject of an <u>infinitive verb</u> takes the objective case.**
This is an exception to the rule that subjects take the nominative case.
> I will hire **whomever** I deem <u>to be</u> the best-qualified applicant.
> I want **him** <u>to have</u> the tickets I cannot use.

Making the Right Choice

In the following practice sentences:

- Bracket the clause or clauses that won't affect the choice between *who* or *whom*. Often such clauses appear at the beginning of the sentence, and the *who/whom* choice relates to a verb that appears later in the sentence.
- Identify the parts of speech in the remaining portion of the sentence, **beginning with the verb.**
- Determine what grammatical function *who* or *whom* will serve. If it serves as the <u>subject</u> or <u>predicate nominative</u>, choose **who** (or other pronoun in the *nominative* case, as indicated by the chart above). If it serves as the <u>direct object</u>, <u>indirect object</u>, <u>object of preposition</u> or <u>subject of infinitive verb</u>, then choose **whom** (or other pronoun in the *objective* case).

Practice Sentences: *Who* vs. *Whom*

1. She knew (who/whom) the lawyers would question first.

    [S   V]   DO   S   V   adv
[She knew] <u>whom</u> the lawyers would question first.

2. I was asked (who/whom) I thought the winner would be.

[S   V]   PN [S V]   S   V
[I was asked] who [I thought] the winner would be.

3. Olivia was determined to find out (who/whom) her admirer was.

[S   V   V]   PN   S   V
[Olivia was determined to find out] who her admirer was.

4. NASA took (whoever/whomever) would volunteer for the mission.

[S   V]   S   V   [prep   OP]
[NASA took] whoever would volunteer [for the mission].

5. Robertson was the candidate (who/whom) the Independents nominated.

[S   V   PN]   DO   S   V
[Robertson was the candidate] whom the Independents nominated.

6. We believed (he/him) to be the best choice.

[S   V]   S inf V   PN
[We believed] him to be the best choice. *(subject of infinitive verb takes objective case)*

7. To (who/whom) do you wish to speak?

prep OP   [V S V   V]
To whom [do you wish to speak]?

8. (Who/whom) should I say is calling?

S   [V S V]   V
Who [should I say] is calling?

Other Rules and Guidelines

Subject-Verb Agreement

prepositional phrase separating subject from verb

Prepositional phrases (indicated in parentheses below) can separate subjects and verbs, causing trouble.

Jinxed by **a series** (of near disasters) (in the last six months) that **includes** two fires, the first collision in orbit, loss of oxygen and several power failures, Mir suffered crises that raised serious questions about the future of manned space flight.

The verb *includes* must agree with the subject *a series*, which is singular — not with *disasters* and/or *months*.

> The **smell** (of freshly baked bread and cakes) **mingles** with the smells of vegetables, meat and fish.

The verb *mingles* must agree with the singular subject *smell* — not with *cakes*.

one of those who/that

In these constructions **the verb agrees with the antecedent (preceding word) of the relative pronoun** — not with *one* — and thus always is plural. In other words, identify the relative pronoun (*who, that, which*), back up one word to its antecedent and make the verb agree with it.

> Stone is one of those **directors who favor** historical topics.

> Where Arabs and Jews live in Jerusalem is a critical issue because it is one of those basic **points that divide** Israeli and Palestinian negotiators: who controls Jerusalem.

> Oprah Winfrey is one of those handful of **entertainers who have** carved such unique places for **themselves** that it is almost impossible to imagine the entertainment landscape without **them**.

collective nouns

Company, team and *group* take singular verbs and pronouns. Team names that are plural or have no plural forms also take plural verbs and pronouns.

> The team is considering its options.
>
> The Bulls and the Magic are considering their options.

either ... or neither ... nor

These **correlative conjunctions** require the verb to agree with the element of the subject closest to it. Reverse the order of the subjects, and a different verb is warranted.

> Either the whale or the **dolphins are** the best exhibit at the aquarium.
>
> Either the dolphins or the **whale is** the best exhibit at the aquarium.

> Neither cake nor **doughnuts are** permitted on your diet.
>
> Neither doughnuts nor **cake is** permitted on your diet.

- Don't separate elements of the verb.
- Keep elements of the correlative conjunctions *either/or,*
  neither/nor and *not only/but also* (*also* is required) as near
  to each other in the sentence as possible.

> *Not:* We **will either buy** the Porsche or the Corvette.
>
> *But:* We **will buy either** the Porsche or the Corvette.

> *Not:* We **will neither accept** your terms nor your conditions.
>
> *But:* We **will accept neither** your terms nor your conditions.

> *Not:* I **will not only accept** my award but yours.
>
> *But:* I **will accept not only** my award but **also** yours.

none

None can take a singular or plural verb depending on the
sense in which it is used. Don't memorize a rule — scrutinize
the context.

- When *none* is used in the sense of **not one**, use a **singular** verb.
- When *none* is used in the sense of **no two** (or more), use
  a **plural** verb.

> All the union members were picketing, but **none** (*not one*)
> **was** paid to be there.
>
> **None** (*not one*) of our neighbors **is** supporting the
> referendum.
>
> **None** of the parties **agree**.
> *(It takes at least two parties to agree with each other.)*
>
> **None** (*not one*) of the parties **agrees** to the proposal.
> *("To the proposal" is key here.)*
>
> **None** of the teams in the league **play** today.
> *(It takes two teams to play.)*

couple

When used in the sense of two people, use a plural verb.
When used in the sense of a single unit, use a singular verb.

> The couple were married in a church.
>
> Each couple was asked to donate $50 to the church fund.

Subject-Pronoun Agreement

switching from singular to plural in midstream

Subjects and pronouns should agree in number throughout the sentence.

> The object is to have three standup comics each try to make **a contestant** laugh, with **that contestant** getting a buck for each second **they** remain stone-faced.

> *Recast:* The object is to have three standup comics each try to make **the contestants** laugh. **They** get a buck for each second **they** remain stone-faced.

everyone, everybody/ gender

Everyone and *everybody* sound plural, but they take **singular verbs and pronouns**. Thus there is a lack of pronoun agreement in

> The teacher told **everyone** to try **their** hardest.

How to recast? If the context is clear that *everyone* refers to one gender, then replace *their* with *his* or *her*. If the gender context is unclear, or if it is known that both sexes are being addressed, then avoid the awkward *his or her* by replacing *everyone* with a plural referent for *their*:

> The teacher told **all of them** to try **their** hardest.
> The teacher told **them all** to try **their** hardest.

Also, consider the inclusive nature of *everyone* and *everybody*:

> He ran faster than everyone on the field.

The problem here is that *he* is included in *everyone*. Recast:

> He ran faster than everyone else on the field.
> *or:* He was the fastest runner on the field.

pronouns refer to nouns, not to possessives

Pronouns must refer to the noun that precedes them. Below, *he* refers to *arm*.

> Although the welder's arm ached, he pushed himself to finish the job.

> *Recast:* Although his arm ached, the welder pushed himself to finish the job.

Misplaced Modifiers

These err in not pointing clearly and directly to what they are supposed to modify. They commonly occur in introductory phrases and clauses, known as *dangling participles*.

> *Rites for Gandhi:* Relatives of Mahatma Gandhi take the ashes of the founding father of India for immersion Thursday in the sacred Ganges River in Allahabad. **Assassinated in 1948**, his ashes had been kept in a vault.

The man was assassinated in 1948, not his ashes.

> *Recast:* … His ashes had been kept in a vault since he was assassinated in 1948.

> *Wrong:* Swimming in the ocean, the boat sailed past me. *(Was the boat swimming?)*
> *Right:* The boat sailed past me as I was swimming in the ocean.

> *Wrong:* Jimmy Carter was the first Georgia governor to be elected president in 1976. *(The first of many that year?)*
> *Right:* In 1976 Jimmy Carter became the first governor of Georgia to be elected president.

Lay *vs.* Lie

The verbs *to lay* and *to lie* have different meanings but confusingly similar forms in different tenses.

	to LAY (to place) *transitive:* takes direct object	**to LIE (to recline)** *intransitive:* does not take direct object
present tense	lay / lays	lie / lies
past tense	laid	lay
present participle	am / is / are laying	am / is / are lying
past participle	have / had laid	have / had lain

> I laid the papers on the table yesterday; today I cannot find them.
> Serena lay down hoping her headache would go away.
> In my dream I am lying on the beach in Barbados.

Relative Pronouns

**that, which,
who, whom**

- Use *who* and *whom* to refer to people and animals with names.

> Krupke is the police officer who arrested me.
>
> Buddy is the Labrador whom the Clintons adopted.
>
> Buddy is the Labrador who is the Clintons' new pet.

- Use *that* and *which* to refer to inanimate objects and unnamed animals.

> This is the rabbit that is destroying my garden.
>
> The rabbit, which is destroying my garden, has brown fur.

- Use *that* without commas for essential clauses or phrases.
- Use *which* with commas for nonessential clauses or phrases.

> The book that I lent you is worth $2,000.
>
> *or:* The book I lent you is worth $2,000.
> *(Drop emphasis by omitting relative pronoun.)*
>
> The book, which I lent you, is worth $2,000.

- In general don't use *that* after *said* unless it is preceded by a time element or followed by a conjunction such as *after, although, because, before, until* or *while.*

> Delgado said he would submit the budget to the City Council.
>
> Delgado said Monday that he would revise the budget.
>
> Delgado said that after he fired his press secretary, he had second thoughts.

- **Avert ambiguity**. Technically the relative pronouns *which* and *that* refer to their antecedents. Thus in the sentence

> The students slept during class, which angered the teacher.

the word *which* technically refers to *class*. Obviously, the meaning is clear from the context: The teacher was bugged by the students' *sleeping*, not by the *class*. Recast any of several ways:

The students slept during class, and that angered the teacher. *(formulate second clause)*

The students slept during class, angering the teacher.

The students' sleeping during class angered the teacher. *(note apostrophe)*

The teacher was angry because the students slept during class.

Miscellany

a, an

Use *a* before words that begin with **consonants** or vowels that have **consonant sounds**.

Use *an* before words that begin with **vowels** or consonants that have **vowel sounds.**

The American Revolution was a historic event. (*an historic* is British usage)

This is a once-in-a-lifetime opportunity.

The firing was an onerous decision.

My father-in-law is an honorable man.

ambiguity

Sometimes repetition or restructuring is necessary to avert ambiguity.

The players honored their coaches and recalled their most brilliant moments of the season.

To whose brilliant moments does the second *their* refer, the players' or the coaches'? Recast accordingly.

The players honored their coaches and recalled the coaches' most brilliant moments of the season.

The players honored their coaches and recalled the team's most brilliant moments of the season.

as ... as
vs.
so ... as

Choose according to whether a positive or negative comparison is being made. When comparing things to show that they are **equal** or **equivalent**, use *as ... as.*

I am as tall as Bill.

When comparing things to show that they are **unequal** or **not equivalent**, use *so ... as*.

> I am not so rich as Bill.
>
> I am as tall as Bill but not so rich as he.

better than I
vs.
better than me

The choice depends on the intended meaning. Both are plausible, but *better than I* is much more likely. Either way, it's *than*, not *then*.

> You like football better than I.
> *(You like the game better than I like the game.)*
>
> You like football better than me.
> *(You like the game better than you like me as a person.)*

between you and me

While *between you and I* may sound grammatical, correct grammar is *between you and me*, because *me* is the object of the preposition *between*.

> Between you and me, I like football better than I like Joe.

feel bad, feel badly

Again, choice depends on intended meaning, but *feel bad* is more likely. Use *bad* as a predicate adjective with *feel* to convey **emotion**.

> I feel bad for you because you have frostbite.

Use the adverb *badly* with *feel* to denote **the tactile act of touching**.

> I felt badly for you with my frostbitten fingers.

good
vs.
well

Good is an adjective or predicate adjective used for descriptive purposes. *Well* is an adverb often used specifically to indicate state of health.

> You look good in that new blue suit.
>
> You're looking well now that you're over your cold.
>
> It's a good thing that Jason plays the piano well.

to grieve
vs. **to mourn**

The death of Princess Diana elicited this headline:
Grieving 'the people's princess'

That, however, would have been impossible, as *grieving* in its transitive form means "to cause to feel grief; afflict with acute sorrow or distress." Because Diana already was dead, correct grammar would have required:

> Mourning 'the people's princess'
> *or:* Grieving for 'the people's princess'

like
vs. **as**

Use the preposition *like* to compare nouns and pronouns. Use the conjunction *as* to introduce clauses.

> Richard raced down the highway like a madman.
>
> Richard slowed down when he saw the police car as he didn't want to get a speeding ticket.

media

When referring to mass communication, among other uses, the noun *media* takes a **plural** verb.

> U.S. media are increasingly corporate-owned.

a number of

When *number* is used in the sense of more than one person or thing, use a plural verb.

> A number of students were protesting the controversial speaker.
>
> A number of books were missing from the library.
>
> The winning lotto number was announced yesterday.

pronouns:
personal *vs.*
possessive

Use the **personal** pronoun when the emphasis is on the *person*. Use the **possessive** pronoun when the emphasis is on the *action*.

> I appreciate him lending me the money — what a good friend!
>
> His lending me the money was a noble gesture.

When the context has no particular emphasis, use the **possessive** pronoun.

> I appreciate his lending me the money.

worse *vs.*
worst

Worst comes to *worst* is technically correct; *worse* comes to *worst* is increasingly accepted usage. Furthermore, *worst* is the **superlative** form, used to compare three or more people or things; *worse* is the **comparative** form, used to compare two. Thus the headline

> Which is worse: Men, bacteria or daytime TV?

should have read

> Which is worst: Men, bacteria or daytime TV?

Verb choices

can *vs.* **may**

The distinction between *can* and *may* in spoken language has all but disappeared. However, in written language, use *can* to denote **ability**, *may* to denote **possibility** or **permission**.

> You can pass the test if you study for it.
>
> The board will make an exception: You may take the test at a later date.
>
> Do you think Lindenbaum can win the election?
>
> Lindenbaum may win the election if rural districts favor him.

shall *vs.* **will**

According to AP, use *shall* to express **determination**. Use *shall* or *will* for first-person constructions that don't emphasize determination. Use *will* for second- and third-person constructions unless determination is stressed.

> I shall help you, and we shall overcome.
>
> We shall attend the seminar. *or:* We will attend the seminar.
>
> You will like the result, but he will not be pleased by it.

should
vs. **would**

Use *should* to express **obligation**.
Use *would* to express **a customary action** or **a conditional past tense**.

> I should have visited my ailing grandfather more often.
>
> As a child, I would visit my grandfather for a month every summer.
>
> If my grandfather had not smoked, he likely would have lived longer.

subjunctive:
was *vs.* **were**

Use *were* to express the **subjunctive** mood for conditions that are contrary to fact or unlikely to happen. Use *was* to indicate conditions that could happen but may not or won't happen.

> If I were you, I'd return those shoes.
>
> If I were going to Zanzibar, I'd buy you a giraffe.
>
> If I was going to the store, I'd pick up a few things for you. But I'm going to Zanzibar.

GRAMMAR SELF-TEST I

Choose the correct answer in the following sentences. *Key on p. 78.*

1. This is the man (who / whom) lives next door.

2. (Who / whom) was the first man on the moon?

3. The committee believed (she / her) to be the best choice.

4. The police knew (who / whom) they would question first.

5. I was asked (who / whom) I thought would win the race.

6. The reporter was determined not to tell (who / whom) her source was.

7. Priyanka is the writer (who / whom) will be nominated for the award.

8. The reporter interviewed (whoever / whomever) would talk on the record.

9. The photographer works with (whoever / whomever) the agency recommends.

10. If I (was / were) French, I could translate the novel easily.

11. Anderson was the candidate (who / whom) the Independent Party chose.

12. I appreciate (you / your) giving the workers time off — what a generous employer!

13. Streep is one of those actors who (is / are) able to do accents well.

14. (Who / Whom) will I know is the right man?

15. To (who / whom) should I address my question?

16. Jay is a craftsman (who / that) takes pride in getting the details right.

17. I am not (as / so) patient as you are.

18. I believe that (you / your) repaying the loan will improve our relationship.

19. These are the pandas (who / that) the zoo recently acquired.

20. There are no secrets between you and (I / me).

GRAMMAR SELF-TEST II

Edit these sentences to correct grammar errors. *Do not rewrite.* If a sentence is correct as is, mark it "OK." If a sentence is ambiguous and more information is needed to fix it, circle the ambiguous element. If it can be corrected by logical inference, do so. *Key on p. 79.*

1. A number of reporters was assigned to cover the convention.

2. He worked at a slower pace than anyone in the class.

3. I feel badly for him.

4. The building has 50 offices, and all but one have gray carpet. The one which is the biggest is the president's office. The business office which has no windows is the smallest.

5. The defense of Tinker, Evers and Chance are unbeatable.

6. Smith told Jones he would paint his car.

7. None of the parties agrees to this proposal.

8. Either the dogs or the cat is bound to run away.

9. Ariel laid down to take a nap but slept until the next morning.

10. The BP oil spill was an historic event.

11. The students applauded their teachers and recalled their best moments in the classroom.

12. None of our tax returns have been audited.

13. The computers which you will find here have the latest operating system.

14. Olga likes to skate better then me.

15. I lay my keys on the table yesterday; today I cannot find it.

16. Although the lawyer's calendar was full, he made time for pro bono clients.

17. Jonas will not only accept his award but my award.

18. None of the parties to the conflict agrees.

19. We will either vacation in Hawaii or in Acapulco.

20. The team played without discipline, which bothered the coach.

21. All 15 pilots attended the seminar, but none was enthusiastic about it.

22. The police officers told everyone to lay their weapons down.

23. Bending in the breeze, I saw the tall trees.

24. The academy submitted their list of candidates.

25. Etta Jones was the first woman to be elected mayor of Manleyville in 2011.

Usage

Usage is the art of using the right word (or its preferred form) in the right place. Unlike punctuation and grammar, the rules for which are relatively finite, usage is a field as broad as the language itself. A discussion of some commonly troublesome usage points follows. To avert usage problems:

- Understand what common errors are and how to correct them.
- Check definitions and word forms in the dictionary when in doubt.
- Consult the stylebook frequently for its dozens of usage entries.

Rules and Guidelines

abortion Outside of direct quotes and names of organizations, steer clear of value-laden terms that often accompany the abortion debate. Use **anti-abortion** rather than *pro-life*; **pro-abortion rights** instead of *pro-choice* or *pro-abortion*.

> Anti-abortion demonstrators picketed the clinic;
> abortion-rights advocates staged a counterdemonstration.
> *("Advocates" makes "pro" prefix redundant.)*

affect, effect Both words can be used as nouns or as verbs. As a noun *affect* means emotion (as in *affection*); as a noun *effect* means result.

> The patient exhibited a low level of affect.
>
> The net effect was a drop in sales.

Confusion often arises when these words are used as verbs. As a verb *affect* means to influence; as a verb *effect* means to bring about or to cause and is often paired with *change*.

> Your pleading will not affect my decision at all.
>
> The candidate vowed to effect change.

among, between Use *between* to refer to two people or things, *among* to refer to three or more. *(See AP stylebook for exception.)*

> You and I will divide the profits between us.
>
> John, Jane and Jim divided the profits among themselves.

anticipate, expect

To *expect* means to look forward to something as likely to happen; to *anticipate* means to expect something to happen *and* to prepare for it.

> We expected a warm August but not a deadly heat wave.
>
> We bought an air conditioner because we anticipated a heat wave.

anxious, eager

Eager implies desire; *anxious* may imply desire but always implies anxiety or worry.

> After a long, cold winter, Regina was eager for spring.
>
> After a long, cold winter, Regina was anxious about her rosebushes.

as ... as

Remember to complete the set and include the second *as*.

> *Not:* My barbecue sauce is as good or better than yours.
>
> *But:* My barbecue sauce is as good as or better than yours.

attribution

The preferred order for simple attribution is **subject-verb**.

> "I'll make you an offer you can't refuse," the godfather said.

Save the verb-subject construction for attributions that are followed by titles, appositive phrases or nonessential phrases.

> "I take full responsibility for the blackout," said Robertson, chairman of the power company since May.
>
> "I take full responsibility for the blackout," said Robertson, who has been chairman of the power company since May.

avert, avoid

To *avert* is to prevent; to *avoid* is to evade.

> Due to Sally's quick thinking, disaster was averted.
>
> I avoided making eye contact with Sally at the party.

a while, awhile

A while is a **noun** meaning a period of time.
Awhile is an **adverb** meaning *for a time* or *for a while*.

> I can wait for a while for Henry to pay me back.
>
> Henry said he would wait awhile to pay me back.

because of, due to

Use *due to* to modify a **noun**.
Use *because of* to modify a **verb**.

> The postponement was due to rain.
>
> The game was postponed because of rain.

cement, concrete

Cement is an ingredient that yields *concrete*.

> The construction company donated 50 barrels of cement.
>
> The builder guaranteed the concrete foundation for 100 years.

champing at the bit

This idiom means to be impatient, restless or very eager for something to happen. **Chomping** *at the bit* is simply incorrect.

> The students were champing at the bit to finish finals and start vacation.

collide

For two objects to *collide*, both must be moving on impact.

> The cars collided on the expressway.
>
> The van crashed into the storefront.

compare with, compare to

Use *compare with* to emphasize differences between like things. Use *compare to* to liken different types of things for effect or to liken two similar things of significantly different quality.

> I compared my garden with yours.
>
> You compared your garden to paradise.
>
> Shelley compared her writing with Tom's.
>
> Tom compared his writing to Shakespeare's.

comprise, compose

Both *comprise* and *compose* mean to embrace, include all or make up — but *comprise* is the more particular of the two. *Is comprised of* is never correct. Furthermore, the whole comprises the parts: The collective noun must precede the constituent parts.

> *Not:* Five men and seven women comprise the jury.
>
> *But:* The jury comprises five men and seven women.
>
> *Or:* The jury is composed of five men and seven women.
>
> *Or:* Five men and seven women compose/make up the jury.

connote, denote

To *connote* means to suggest or to imply beyond an explicit meaning. To *denote* means to give an explicit meaning.

> Avoid the word "claimed" unless you want to connote doubt.
>
> Use the word "starving" to denote extreme hunger.

continual, continuous

Continual means steadily repeated.
Continuous means uninterrupted or unbroken.

> Ruth found a continual source of happiness in her grandchildren's visits.
>
> Jeremy experienced continuous neck pain for two months after the car accident.

convince, persuade

You *convince* someone to believe a certain thing but *persuade* someone to take a certain action. Note the companion words: *convince* **that** and *persuade* **to**.

> I will convince you that I am right.
>
> I will persuade you to vote for me.

a couple of

Always include *of.* And because this phrase denotes two of something, don't make the inaccurate substitution of *a few*, which denotes three or more.

> A couple of sunny days are all it will take for the flowers to bloom.

declined to, refused to

Declined to means "no"; *refused to* means "hell, no" and requires a more specific, emphatic context. Saying someone refused to comment when she merely declined implies that perhaps she is hiding something. Thus use *refused to* sparingly and with greater care relative to context.

Also, the verb *to comment* is infinitive: *Refused comment* and *declined comment* (without *to*) are incorrect.

> The president declined to comment on whether he would veto the bill.
>
> Five reporters asked the same question, but the president refused to comment.

different from, differ from

Different takes the preposition *from*, not *than* — just as *to differ from* means to be unlike.

> Mary's opinion is different from George's.
>
> Mary's opinion differs from George's.

disburse, disperse

To *disburse* means to distribute. To *disperse* means to scatter.

> The IRS will be late in disbursing tax refunds this year.
>
> My best friend's family is dispersed throughout the country.

discreet, discrete

Discreet means judicious or careful.
Discrete means separate or distinct.

> The reporter interviewed the prosecutor off the record in a discreet meeting.
>
> The prosecutor outlined three discrete tactics she would use to try the case.

each other, one another

Use *each other* to refer to two people; use *one another* to refer to three or more. Either may be used to refer to an indefinite number.

> You and I will help each other; the rest of the group will help one another.
>
> We don't know when we will see each other/one another again.

ensure, insure

Use *ensure* to mean to guarantee; use *insure* for references to insurance.

> Steps were taken to ensure the president's safety.
>
> The policy insures my car for collision damage, less a $250 deductible.

farther, further

For measurable physical distance, use *farther*. For abstractions use *further*.

> Lisa ran farther than Jamie.
>
> Jamie refused to discuss the matter further with Lisa.
>
> If you need a great used car, look no further.

fewer, less   If you can count items individually, use *fewer*. If not use *less*.

> The express line is for people with 10 items or fewer.
>
> If I had fewer deadlines, I would feel less pressured.

flaunt, flout   To *flaunt* is to show off; to *flout* is to mock or show contempt.

> Buffy flaunted her new sports car, racing down Lake Shore Drive at 80 mph.
>
> Buffy learned the price of flouting the speed limit: an $80 traffic ticket.

hanged, hung   Use *hanged* in reference to executions and suicides, *hung* for pictures and other actions.

> Robertson hanged himself after squandering his entire fortune.
>
> Johnson hung his head in grief when he learned of Robertson's suicide.

hopefully   *Hopefully* can mean "in a hopeful manner" (traditional usage) or "it is hoped/we hope" (modern usage). Both of the following are correct; note comma in the second example.

> "You'll come to the party with me?" Jenna asked hopefully.
>
> Hopefully, we'll see you soon.

immigrate, emigrate   One *immigrates* **to** a country and *emigrates* **from** a country.

> The Ryans immigrated to the United States during the potato famine.
>
> Record numbers emigrated from Ireland during the potato famine.

imply, infer	**Speakers** and **writers** *imply*; **listeners** and **readers** *infer*.

> In her statement to police, Jeanette implied that she knew the killer's identity.
>
> After hearing the defendant testify, Jeanette inferred that he was innocent.

include	To *include* implies a **partial** list.

> *Not:* The trio includes a soprano, a tenor and a baritone.
>
> *But:* The trio comprises a soprano, a tenor and a baritone.
>
> *Or:* The trio is composed of a soprano, a tenor and a baritone.
>
> ✔ The zoo includes reptile and butterfly exhibits.

irregardless	This is an incorrect double negative; use *regardless*.

> *Wrong:* You won't persuade me to go irregardless of the incentives you offer.
>
> *Right:* You can't convince me that you are right regardless of your argument.

its, it's	This one bears repeating: *Its* is the **possessive** form of *it*. *It's* is a **contraction** meaning *it is*. (*See* **Punctuation**; **Apostrophes**.)

> The restaurant doubled its business after it got a favorable review.
>
> It's the best Lebanese restaurant within a 50-mile radius.

lend, loan	Use *lend* as a **verb** and *loan* as a **noun**.

> Joyce said she'll lend me her car if I give her a $50 loan.

loath, loathe	*Loath* is an adjective meaning reluctant; *loathe* is a verb meaning to dislike intensely or to hate.

> I am loath to tell you that I loathe your new tie.

majority, plurality	*Majority* means more than half of an amount. *Plurality* means more than the next-highest number or the highest number when a majority is not attainable.

> Ella received a plurality of the votes with 48 of 100 cast; Jose got 33 and Miko, 19.

mishap

Mishaps are minor misfortunes that do not include death or serious injury.

> *Not:* My neighbor died in a traffic mishap.
>
> *But:* My neighbor suffered a series of mishaps with his car before he died in a traffic accident.

more than, over

AP style no longer distinguishes between *more than* and *over* to indicate greater numerical value. Both of the following are correct:

> More than 10,000 people attended the concert.
>
> Over 10,000 people attended the concert.

only

The placement of *only* can affect the meaning of a sentence.

> This is the **only** movie I want to see.
> *(I'm a very discriminating filmgoer.)*
>
> This is the movie **only** I want to see.
> *(Looks like I'll be going alone.)*

onto, on to

Onto is a spatial reference; *on to* refers to awareness of real nature or meaning.

> Put a stamp onto the letter, or the post office won't deliver it.
>
> When I read your letter, I caught on to your desire to work at the post office.

past, experience

Use one or the other; together they are redundant.

> Nothing in my past prepared me for this.
>
> Nothing in my experience prepared me for this.

plethora

Plethora doesn't mean abundance — it means overabundance. The sentence

> A plethora of students wanted to take the popular film course.

means that some would be disappointed because there were too many students for too few spaces.

presently   Use *presently* to mean in a little while or soon, *currently* to mean now.

> We expect that the announcement will be made presently.
>
> We are currently waiting for the announcement to be made.

rebuke, rebut, refute   To *rebuke* is to express sharp disapproval or criticism. To *rebut* is merely to challenge or to dispute; to *refute* is to go a step further and to disprove a theory or to prevail in an argument.

> The president rebuked Republican senators for their latest filibuster.
>
> The reader rebutted the critic's review.
>
> The prosecutor refuted the defense's theory and won a conviction.

respectively   *Respectively* forces the reader to double back, as in

> Sheridan Road will be closed for repairs in Evanston and Chicago on Monday and Tuesday, respectively.

Recast to omit *respectively* and to put related elements together, repeating the prepositions *in* and *on* for the sake of parallel construction.

> Sheridan Road will be closed for repairs in Evanston on Monday and in Chicago on Tuesday.
>
> Sheridan Road will be closed for repairs on Monday in Evanston and on Tuesday in Chicago.

review, revue   A *review* can be an evaluation, re-examination or inspection. A *revue* is a variety show.

> Michael got a hefty raise after an excellent annual review.
>
> Michaela got hefty praise for her performance in the annual revue.

said, claimed, admitted   Save verbs like *claimed* and *admitted* for specific contexts in which dispute or guilt may be a factor. Otherwise, use *said*.

> The defendant claimed throughout the trial that he was innocent.
>
> The suspect admitted to police that he had held a grudge against the victim.
>
> Hans said he got a good deal on the BMW.

some

Use *some* when a colloquial tone is called for.

> The whittler recalled that he took up the craft some 50 years ago.
>
> *Not:* Some 20,000 people were killed in the earthquake.
>
> *But:* Approximately/An estimated 20,000 people were killed in the earthquake.

Note that merely deleting *some* changes an approximation to an exact figure, which most likely is incorrect.

strangled to death

If one is strangled, then one is likely dead. This is not necessarily so, though, with choking.

> *Not:* Jones was found strangled to death.
>
> *But:* Jones was found strangled.
>
> *Or:* The medical examiner said Jones had choked to death.

suddenly, unexpectedly

Everyone dies *suddenly.*
Those who are not acutely or chronically ill die *unexpectedly.*

> The athlete died unexpectedly.
>
> The athlete died of a sudden illness.
>
> The athlete's death was unexpected.

totally destroyed, demolished

Destruction has totality built in; so does *demolition.*
Damage may equal destruction to a part of the whole.

> *Not:* The mansion was totally destroyed by fire.
>
> *But:* The mansion was destroyed by fire.
>
> *Not:* The earthquake demolished part of the building.
>
> *But:* The earthquake demolished the building.
>
> *Or:* The earthquake damaged part of the building.
>
> The mansion had extensive fire damage, with its west wing destroyed.
>
> Damage from the fire totaled $1 billion.

unique

Unique needs no embellishment, emphasis or modification. It means "one of a kind" or "unparalleled." *Really unique, very unique* and *extremely unique* are all redundant.

> Charlie's writing style is unique.

USAGE SELF-TEST

Edit the following sentences to improve word choice, omit needless words and/or make other corrections as warranted. *Do not rewrite!* Some sentences may be correct as written. *Key on p. 80.*

1. Jones's approach is different than his wife's.
2. The Norrises' neighbor was found strangled to death.
3. We did not anticipate that the club would sell it's membership list to telemarketers.
4. Jimmy could not convince the car dealer to ignore his credit report, said his wife.
5. His approach to the problem is extremely unique.
6. If I had less problems, I would be less depressed.
7. The CEO died suddenly without having named a successor.
8. The fire totally destroyed the house, which was worth some $300,000.
9. The president only refused comment on the plan to invade Tobago.
10. I compared my test results to my roommate.
11. Nine blacks, two whites and a Latino comprised the jury.
12. From what you said, I implied that you'll come to my party.
13. Charlotte inferred discretely that she would run for the school board.
14. Roger vowed to run as fast or faster then his rival.
15. A couple more laps and you will be finished with practice.
16. The class was postponed for over a week due to the teacher's illness.
17. I have traveled further than you but have visited less countries.
18. Walid claimed that he had never met the man.
19. The student driver collided with the stop sign.
20. The candidate continuously refuted her opponent's charges.
21. After not eating for seven hours, Jerry was anxious to have dinner.
22. The food pantry dispersed a plethora of canned goods to the city's 10,000 homeless.
23. The new administration is anticipated to affect change.
24. Your preparation will effect your ability to perform well.
25. The first day of school in Milwaukee and the northern suburbs will be Tuesday and Wednesday, respectively.
26. The three suspects include a doctor, a lawyer and an accountant.
27. The jurors were chomping at the bit to reach a verdict so they could go home.
28. Tonya's past experience abroad has helped her to understand Japanese culture.
29. John Lennon compared his music with the Gospel.
30. The pro-choice rally was held in front of the White House.

RECAP: COMPREHENSIVE SELF-TEST

Edit the following sentences for correct punctuation, grammar and usage. Rewrite only when absolutely necessary, and don't edit out meaning or emphasis. Some sentences contain more than one error. *Key on p. 81.*

1. The candidate vowed to affect change in three areas Health care, the deficit, and education.

2. Last year, I was not as tall as you, but this year I grew more than 6 inches.

3. My friend, Vinnie, compared his real estate taxes to mine.

4. I shopped I charged I owed they billed, they dunned they repossessed. (*Edit as single sentence.*)

5. The couple from Yonkers N.Y. moved to 200 Linden Drive Phoenix on May 4 2010.

6. It was the head nurse that asked "(Who/Whom) is responsible for this mix-up?"

7. My oldest brother David, loves to watch old TV shows including "Mission: Impossible," "Hill Street Blues" and "The Sonny And Cher Show."

8. If I was you, I would not entrust a multi-million dollar project to my brother-in-law.

9. Remember this: the couple was injured because they weren't wearing seat belts.

10. North America is comprised of three countries; Canada, the United States, and Mexico.

11. We looked at first and second floor apartments in the building which you recommended.

12. Roland said, "None of the taxes has been paid. The bank will repossess our farm."

13. What I bought Sally for her birthday he said, is not what she anticipated.

14. The actress declined to answer questions, and she shouted at the reporters to leave her alone.

15. Traveling in Europe, my expensive, leather briefcase was lost.

16. My new car has a dent which bothers me.

17. The neighbors, who live to the south of us, admire our garden.

18. Give (we/us), the student body, lower tuition free parking, and better housing.

19. The gambler lay his cards on the table and said, "Friends I have a royal flush."

20. My new car has a CD player, but not cruise control.

21. "Give the report to (whoever/whomever) you want," the mayor's press secretary said.

22. I must object to (his/him) getting the award, because I deserve it more.

23. The mayor, crushed between her top aides and (I/me), began to panic.

24. You're looking (well/good) — are you over your cold?

25. He wondered (who/whom) he could ask to look into the matter farther.

26. If I (was/were) you, I would demand that your attacker be brought to justice.

27. Pressing their attack, (the mayor was the media's next target/the media made the mayor their next target).

28. It is (we/us) who are the victims.

29. It was (I/me) you saw at the KitKat Club.

30. If you add a couple dried red peppers, your chili will be as hot or hotter then mine.

31. Woody Allen is one of those actors who never (seem/seems) to be at ease on the screen.

32. The president (had only/only had) one option but he described several scenarios.

33. Can you believe that I just (lay/laid) on the beach all summer?

34. There (go/goes) the best team and best coach in baseball.

35. Nobody studied harder than (I/me) for this exam.

36. Northwestern will either play Illinois or Michigan.

37. Neither the coach nor the team (want/wants) to do anything that would hurt the university's image.

38. The couple (was/were) separated for nine hours during the earthquake.

39. I know (who/whom) you think to be the best candidate.

40. Police frisked (whoever/whomever) came through the gate.

41. None of the passengers were injured when the train derailed and collided with the mountain.

42. Be careful: I just might be onto you.

43. This prosecutor would charge (whoever/whomever) walks through that door next if he thought it would advance his career.

44. I agree that (his/him) storming out of the room aggravated the situation, but it did not start the trouble.

45. There has never been (as/so) great an estrangement as there is now between Hannah and her sister.

46. It took awhile, but trust grew between the three of us.

47. None of us (go/goes) out as much as before.

48. Neither of the first-place winners (plan/plans) to donate (her/their) prize money to charity.

49. Repeated mistakes made the teacher grow (quick/quickly) to criticize his students.

50. Just (lay/lie) the book over there and I'll pick it up later.

AP Stylebook Study Guide

The Associated Press Stylebook is the standard reference for media style. Many larger news organizations that have their own stylebooks adopt much of their content from AP. *Be aware that AP updates and adds style entries on an ongoing basis.*

The lists below are designed to impart a working knowledge of the range and types of entries in the AP stylebook on frequently consulted issues.

Consult these stylebook entries for AP Style Self-Test I *(pp. 43–44)*

abbreviations and acronyms	legislative titles	that (conjunction)
addresses	military titles	time element
capitalization	numerals	times
composition titles; newspaper names	organizations and institutions	titles
courtesy titles	people, persons	United Nations
datelines	plurals	U.S.
dimensions	possessives	verbs
directions and regions	state names	years

Consult these stylebook entries for AP Style Self-Test II *(p. 45)*

academic departments	earth	Mass
ages	following	No.
child care	freelancer	on
church	full time, full-time;	police department
city; city council	part time, part-time	prison, jail
committee	fundraising, fundraiser	spokesman,
company names;	gay	spokeswoman
corporation	hotline	youth; boy; girl
department (gov't listings)	illegal immigration	woman, women
doctor; professor	last; late	
drunk, drunken	man, mankind	

Consult these stylebook entries for AP Style Self-Test III *(pp. 46–47)*

African-American; black; race	middle initials	Public Broadcasting
al-Qaida	miles per hour; mph	Service
Commonwealth of Independent States	months	religious references
couple	National Organization	religious titles
foreign legislative bodies	for Women	Sept. 11; 9/11
governmental bodies	Native American; Indians	Teamsters union
Internet; email; offline; online; website	party affiliation	union names
Islam; Muslims; Quran; imam; jihad	percent	U.S. Postal Service
Latino; Hispanic	political parties, philosophies	weapons

AP STYLE SELF-TEST I

Correct the AP style errors in the following sentences. *Do not rewrite.* Some sentences contain more than one error; others may be correct as is. *Key on p. 83.*

1. The blizzard hit the Midwest hardest, particularly Northern Illinois.

2. Public School No. 7 raised the price of lunch to two dollars thirty cents.

3. Sasha and wife Svetlana went camping near Jackson Hole, WY. this summer.

4. The suburban law firm moved downtown to 225 West Washington Street.

5. 1978 was the year John Paul the Second became Pope.

6. NASA was established as the United States space agency in the late 1950's.

7. Derek Johnson reported on Congresswoman Jones until it came out that he had worked for Ms. Jones as an intern.

8. The 6'-11" center was bypassed in the draft for the five-foot-eight-inch guard.

9. During the trial the defendant asserted he did not kill his wife.

10. The storm dumped seven inches of rain on the North Shore suburbs.

11. Natural disasters including earthquakes and mudslides have plagued Southern California in recent years.

12. The 1st Amendment has 45 words contained in one paragraph.

13. CHICAGO, Illinois — A Boston, Mass., man was arrested Tuesday in connection with insider-trading schemes at the Chicago Board of Trade (CBOT).

14. The House voted 300 to 135 to cut $60,000,000,000 from the federal budget.

15. The Lakeview neighborhood association parade route is bounded by Diversey and Belmont Avenues and Halsted and Clark streets.

16. American foreign policy does not always reflect public opinion in the United States.

17. Fritz ordered French fries and a manhattan cocktail.

18. Customs for care of elderly parents in the east differs from such customs in the west.

19. The White House is located at 1600 Pennsylvania Avenue, not far from the offices of the "Washington Post."

20. "Doctor Bond and Governor Cash are ideal candidates for the trade commission," Sen. Steve Stephens said.

21. The Plano, Tx., woman won the lottery while visiting her cousin in Cleveland, Oh.

22. Williams contended her boss owed her two months back pay.

23. Acting mayor Ginger Grant appointed Jonas Grumby Minister of Transportation.

24. Ahmad's two daughter-in-laws were among the passer-bys injured when the van jumped the curb.

25. I put two teaspoonsful of sugar in my coffee.

26. Jodie's mother and aunt are Yale University alumni.

27. The hurricane destroyed the childrens' hospital and the teachers' college.

28. The relationship between social media and traditional media has become a popular topic for many masters' thesis.

29. The Christmas song admonishes: Be good for goodness sake.

30. Herbert Bang is a friend of my father and a supporter of the National Rifle Association's.

31. The deers' tracks led to the Marine Corp's training camp.

32. The Supreme Court is expected to rule at 9:00 a.m. next Monday morning.

33. The scissors is in my desk drawer.

34. Fourteen persons attended the creative-writing workshop.

35. The mumps were the first childhood disease my sister had.

36. The people of the Middle East speak many languages, and their countries are represented in the UN.

37. The second witness' answer contradicted the first witness's story.

38. The property-tax and handgun issues will be voted on in special referenda.

39. The Jones live to the south of us.

40. I had to really guess at what she meant.

41. Ann's home library includes "Webster's New World Dictionary," "The Rise And Fall of The Third Reich" and a worn copy of The Bible.

42. Sergeant Major Lovely commended Privates Fine and Dandy.

43. Xena had usually gone to battle accompanied by Gabrielle.

AP STYLE SELF-TEST II

Correct the AP style errors in the following sentences. *Do not rewrite.* Some sentences contain more than one error. *Key on p. 85.*

1. The English Department offers 20 literature courses each fall.

2. The junior high school principal suspended Monday the girls who played the prank.

3. Mayor Rogers announced Friday Gainesville will make a bid to host the Summer Olympics.

4. The 18 year old youth was the youngest hired by the 100 year old company.

5. The business world was rocked by the merger of First Bank, Ltd. and United Finance Corporation.

6. The late Mickey Mantle hit the most home runs in the American League in 1955.

7. I talked to my cousin last Wednesday about the free-lance article I'm writing.

8. The fund-raising dinner for the new gymnasium was the PTA's number one priority.

9. Gates was in his mid 20s in the mid 70s.

10. The student club's Finance Committee was inspired to do fund raising by the Senate foreign relations committee vote to send aid to Afghanistan.

11. After serving a 15-year jail sentence for armed robbery, Cunningham began working part-time.

12. Saying mass is an important ritual in the Roman Catholic church.

13. Following her drunk driving conviction, Prof. Lori Evans, an attractive blonde, began attending Alcoholics Anonymous meetings.

14. The actor's spokesperson did not return the reporter's phone calls.

15. The Greenville city council has excellent relations with the police department.

16. Marcel got a fulltime job working for the Dept. of Motor Vehicles.

17. In February Lucinda Rodriguez celebrated her tenth year as a practicing physician.

18. A cure for cancer would benefit all mankind.

19. The gay hot line has two full time staffers.

20. Monica moved heaven and Earth to enroll her daughter in the Church child-care program.

AP STYLE SELF-TEST III

Correct the AP style errors in the following sentences. *Do not rewrite.* Some sentences contain more than one error; others may be correct as is. *Key on p. 86.*

1. Some activists still call themselves marxists despite the decline of Communism.

2. The Commonwealth of Independent States comprises the 11 former republics of the U.S.S.R., with Russia as the largest.

3. Many truck drivers belong to the Teamsters' Union.

4. Sam S. Smith was convicted of murder.

5. The September 11, 2001, attacks are thought to be the work of Al Qaida.

6. Jane spends an hour a day on line reading and sending e-mail.

7. We saw the sites of Jesus's Crucifixion and His believed Resurrection on a tour of Jerusalem's Old City.

8. Representatives Jan Bowers [R., Fla.] and Lan Flowers [D., Ark.] co-authored a bipartisan healthcare reform bill.

9. The Federal Deposit Insurance Corporation underwrites some PBS network programming.

10. The resignation of the prime minister caused an uproar in the Knesset, Israel's Parliament.

11. Bill J. Clinton was the first second-term democrat since FDR.

12. Hinckley and Schmidt were among the newsmen assigned to cover the Republican national convention.

13. The U.S. Post Office will raise its rates again next year.

14. Ed's first task as Webmaster is to redesign the company's Web site.

15. Marie's grandparents were married in Jan., 1950, and her mother, Amelia, was born on February 15, 1951.

16. The headquarters of the National Organization of Women is in Washington DC.

17. Rev. Joe Martin traveled to Rome and met the Pope.

18. Only five percent to 10 percent of U.S. highways have speed limits of 65 m.p.h. or higher.

19. Many Whites and Latinos attended the native American culture festival.

20. The police seized a weapons cache that included five 22 caliber rifles and eight 9-mm. pistols.

21. Two of the biggest unions in the United States are the United Autoworkers and the United Steelworkers.

22. African Americans constitute a plurality of the population in many U.S. cities.

23. The couple was married by the Imam.

24. The majority of Moslems are Sunnis; Shi'ites are the largest minority sect. The holy book for both is the Koran.

Spelling

How important is it to know how to spell in the age of spell check?

You can't always rely on the program. Deadlines may not allow time to run it. And not only will spell check *not* save the day when it comes to *there* vs. *their* — but it also can insert errors: You type **Chech Republic** and spell check makes it ***Check Republic***, not ***Czech Republic***.

The AP stylebook lists spellings of places, organizations and other proper nouns along with many other words that are included in the SPELLTRAPS list on pp. 50–52.

When the stylebook offers no guidance, refer to Webster's online dictionary.

When stylebook and dictionary disagree, the stylebook trumps. When the dictionary lists two spellings for the same word, use the first one. This goes for word endings, too. If a word has two separate entries, go with the one that has the definition.

Don't use spellings that are introduced by *also*, *var.* (variation), *alt.* (alternate) or *Brit.* (British).

HOMONYMS AND SOUND-ALIKES EXERCISE

homonym: *n.* a word pronounced the same as another but with a different meaning and usually spelling.

Match the words on the list with their definitions in order to master spellings and meanings alike. Key on p. 87.

1. bloc	11. eek	21. gibe	31. palette	41. ravage
2. block	12. eke	22. hangar	32. pallet	42. ravish
3. complacent	13. flaunt	23. hanger	33. premier	43. riffle
4. complaisant	14. flout	24. jibe	34. premiere	44. rifle
5. complement	15. flounder	25. jive	35. principal	45. secede
6. compliment	16. founder	26. mantel	36. principle	46. succeed
7. consul	17. gambit	27. mantle	37. prostate	47. stanch
8. counsel	18. gamut	28. marshal	38. prostrate	48. staunch
9. disc	19. gantlet	29. martial	39. reign	49. stationary
10. disk	20. gauntlet	30. palate	40. rein	50. stationery

___ **a.** chief official in a consulate

___ **b.** an artist's paint board

___ **c.** official in charge of a procession or ceremony

___ **d.** where an airplane is parked

___ **e.** to praise or flatter

___ **f.** a flogging ordeal, literally or figuratively

___ **g.** to show off or make a gaudy display

___ **h.** lying flat or prone-

___ **i.** to wreak destruction or devastation

___ **j.** writing paper and envelopes

___ **k.** a person first in rank or authority

___ **l.** to leaf rapidly through a book or papers

___ **m.** to withdraw from

___ **n.** a bed, often of wood

___ **o.** to stumble, get bogged down or sink

___ **p.** an alliance or group joined in mutual support

___ **q.** to complete

___ **r.** a first performance

___ **s.** a complete range or extent

___ **t.** a shelf, often over a fireplace

___ **u.** a small frame on which to hang clothing

___ **v.** refers to optical and laser devices and a type of brake

___ **w.** military or warlike in nature

___ **x.** prime minister

___ **y.** a period of rule

___ **z.** to plunder or steal

___ **aa.** to taunt or sneer

___ **bb.** animated expression of shock or surprise

___ **cc.** to show scorn or contempt

___ **dd.** to halt or stop, as in flow of blood

___ **ee.** not moving or movable; fixed or still

___ **ff.** the roof of the mouth

___ **gg.** an opening action to gain advantage

___ **hh.** to speak or act awkwardly

___ **ii.** to abduct, rape or enrapture

___ **jj.** a leather strap for controlling a horse

___ **kk.** literally, a glove; figuratively, a challenge

___ **ll.** a solid piece of material used for support

___ **mm.** to follow or come next after another

___ **nn.** a gland at the base of the bladder in males

___ **oo.** for computer-related and medical references

___ **pp.** to manage (a living) with difficulty

___ **qq.** strong or stalwart

___ **rr.** a fundamental truth or rule of conduct

___ **ss.** eager to please

___ **tt.** to tease, fool or kid

___ **uu.** advice or guidance

___ **vv.** a cape or figurative symbol of authority

___ **ww.** self-satisfied, often smugly so

___ **xx.** to shift direction or to agree with

SPELLTRAPS

Boldface entries on this list of often misspelled words are also AP stylebook entries.

A
accelerate
accessible
accommodate
accordion
accumulate
acquitted
admissible
advantageous
adviser
affidavit
afterward
alleged
allegiance
allotment, **allotted**
all right
a lot (many)
anoint
antidote
antiquated
appall
apparatus
asinine
asphalt
assassinate
assistant
ax

B
backward
bailiff
barbiturate
barroom
battalion
beige
bellwether
benefited, benefiting
berserk
bourgeois

C
caffeine
camaraderie

camouflage
canceled, canceling
cannot
carburetor
caress
cello
cellphone
cemetery
changeable
chaperon
chastise
chauffeur
check-in (*n., adj.*)
checkout (*n., adj.*)
checkup (*n.*)
chili, chilies
cleanup (*n., adj.*)
Cincinnati
Colombia (S. America)
colossal
commemorate
commitment
connoisseur
consensus
consistent
contemptible
contemptuous
corroborate
czar

D
daylong
defendant
definitely
delicatessen
demagogue
dependent
descendant
desirable
desperate
despondent
detrimental
dietitian

dilettante
diphtheria
disastrous
discipline
dismantle
dissension
dissociate
Doberman pinscher
drought
drunken
drunkenness
duffel
dumbbell
dybbuk

E
e-book
ecstasy
email
embarrass
emphysema
enforceable
enroll
entrepreneur
espresso
exhilarate
excerpt
excusable
existence
exonerate
exorbitant
exuberant

F
Fahrenheit
familiar
feasible
fictitious
fidget
firsthand (*adj., adv.*)
flier
fluorescent
flutist

fraudulent
fraught
freelance, freelancer
fulfill
fundraiser, fundraising

G
gaiety
gauge
genealogy
grammar
guarantee
gubernatorial
guerrilla
guttural

H
harangue
harass
health care (*n., adj.*)
hemorrhage
hierarchy
hitchhiker
homicide
hygiene, hygienic

I
icicle
idiosyncrasy
illegible
impostor
impresario
inconceivable
incredible
independent
indestructible
indispensable
innocuous
inoculate
inquire, inquiry
interfered
interrogate
iridescent
irresistible

J
jeopardize
judgment

K
kamikaze
ketchup
kidnapped

L
lascivious
liaison
lieutenant
lightning
likable
livable
liquefy
longtime (*adj.*)

M
maintenance
makeup (*n., adj.*)
manageable
maneuver
marijuana
marriageable
mayonnaise
medieval
memento
miniature
mischievous
miscellaneous
missile
misspell
mix-up (*n.*)
moccasin
monthlong
movable
Muslim

N
naive
naphtha
necessary
negotiable
newsstand
nickel
nighttime
noticeable
nutritious

O
obsolescence
occasionally
occurred
occurrence
OK, OKs, OK'd
ophthalmologist
oscillate

P
pageant
panicked, panicking
pantomime
papier-mâché
parallel, paralleled
paraphernalia
parliament
passers-by
pastime
pavilion
penicillin
penitentiary
percent
peremptory
permanence
permissible
perseverance
persistence
persistent
personnel
Ph.D., Ph.D.s
Philippines
phony
picnicked, picnicking
playwright
politicking
pompom
Post-it
potpourri
preceding
preferable
preference
preferred, preferring
prerogative
presumptuous
privilege
procedure, proceed
pronunciation

propeller
protester
publicly
pullback (*n.*)
pullout (*n.*)

Q
quandary
questionnaire
queue
Quran

R
rarefy
receive
recommend
reconnaissance
referred, referring
reminiscent
renaissance
resistance
resistible
restaurateur
resuscitation
rhythm
riffraff
rip-off (*n., adj.*)
rock 'n' roll
rococo
roundup (*n.*)

S
salable
sapphire
sacrilegious
savior
schizophrenic
schoolteacher
seize

Scotch whisky
screech
secondhand (*adj., adv.*)
second-rate
separate
setup (*n.*)
sheriff
showoff (*n.*)
shutdown (*n.*)
shut-off (*n.*)
siege
silhouette
sizable
skillful
smartphone
smoky
soothe
souvenir
specimen
straight-laced
straitjacket
subpoenaed
superintendent
supersede
surprise
susceptible
swastika

T
tariff
teenage, teenager
terrific
threshold
tiptop
titillate
tortoise
toward
traveled, traveling
T-shirt

tumultuous
twelfth

U
underway
undoubtedly
unmistakable
usable

V
vaccine
vacuum
vaudeville
vengeance
vermilion
Veterans Day
vice versa
vigilance
vilify
villain
volatile
vuvuzela

W
weird
whiskey
wield
withhold
wondrous
wrongdoing

Y
yacht
yearlong
yield
YouTube

Z
zigzag

Copy-Editing Symbols

Copy-editing symbols are still in use — even as editing on paper is done less and less frequently. The symbols denote intended changes clearly and economically.

COPY-EDITING SYMBOLS SELF-TEST

Use the symbols on the next page to edit the following sentences according to AP style. *Key on p. 88.*

1. The expensive, leather briefcase was made in N.J.

2. The stunning long coat is made of 100 per cent cashmere.

3. It has been a years time since I hearrd "be good for goodness sake."

4. I have an idea you may not like it that I think will work.

5. Karim enrolled in the teachers' college.

6. Mr. Jones is survived by his wife, Jana; a son, John, and a daughter, Joan.

7. Mr. Jones is survived by his wife, Jana; and a son, John.

8. The two hour play was badly-acted and and very dull.

9. The Pope will Chicago visit netx week.

10. The mass will be said at 11 a.m. in Saint Mark's Church.

11. The new ambasader will asume her duties on October 15th.

12. "Take my advice and don't buy that cat Jesse's father said.

13. The prescription for good health is threefold Proper diet, exercise, and sufficient rest.

14. "Can you give me a few [minutes to get ready" Ellen asked.

■ Basic Symbolism

abbreviate / spell out

(Ill.) = Illinois   (Illinois) = Ill.   (twelve) = 12   (12) = twelve

insert hyphen   *insert dash*   *insert period*   *insert comma*   *capitalize*   *lowercase*

  =̲   ⊢—⊣   ⊗ or ⊙   ⌃   m̲̲ = M   M̸ = m

CHICAGO⊢After(twenty) years in office, Richard M. Daley, the most well-known politician in(Ill.)announced Wednesday that he would not seek reelection as Mayor of chicago.

split one paragraph into two

CHICAGO — Like father, like son. Mayor Richard M. Daley announced Wednesday that he would not run again after serving six terms in office, as many as his father did.

transpose letters / words

The quick bowrn fox over jumped the lazy dog.

insert space between words

The quick brown fox jumped over the lazy dog.

delete extraneous letters / words

Northwesstern University (stet) is the city of Evanston's largest employer.

insert missing letters / words

The quikfox jumped o̸er thedog.   The quikfox jumped o̸er thedog.
(brown, lazy)   (c brown, lazy)

miscellaneous

CQ = correct as is   **stet** = let original stand >>> dog (stet) = dog
(further checking is unnecessary)

Supplementary Self-Tests

PUNCTUATION/AP STYLE TEST

Edit the following sentences for punctuation and AP style. *Key on p. 89.*

1. Chop some wood or we won't be able to make a fire.

2. The president read his statement, and left the briefing room without taking questions.

3. The meeting will be chaired by three Department Heads Mark Sparks, engineering Bill Cash finance and Faith Morrow development.

4. The Congressional delegation visited the disaster site, the governor stayed away. *(Punctuate as a single sentence.)*

5. Leslie had homework but she didn't feel like doing it.

6. Lowell was the best designer on the team, or he thought he was.

7. A good editor needs 3 skills speed, accuracy, and diplomacy.

8. Working through the bureaucracy is a long tiresome process.

9. Marlo prefers well known brands which are usually more expensive.

10. Cigarette packages carry this warning (among others) "Cigarette Smoke Contains Carbon Monoxide".

11. The CEO announced her retirement, and then she took questions from reporters.

12. Reggie invited his oldest sister Rana and her husband Ralph to the party.

13. After hurricane Katrina, the south will never be the same.

14. I gave my grandmother's necklace which is one hundred years-old to my 13 year old daughter.

15. Jimmy went on a diet, lost a lot of weight, and bought new clothes.

GRAMMAR/AP STYLE TEST

Correct the following sentences for grammar and AP style errors. When called for, circle the right choice. If a sentence is correct as is, mark it "OK." *Key on p. 90.*

1. The police considered (he/him) to be the primary suspect.

2. The jigsaw puzzle which Ryan brought over yesterday is still in the box.

3. The police asked everyone who had witnessed the accident for their phone numbers.

4. The Apollo 11 moon landing was an historic event.

5. The scout asked the coach (who/whom) he thought was the most versatile player.

6. None of the economic experts surveyed agree that a massive tax cut is good policy.

7. Peanut brittle is one of those sweets that (is/are) especially hard on the teeth.

8. The Committee knew (who/whom) it would question first.

9. Makiko likes stock-car racing more then her.

10. I layed the reports on my desk yesterday but couldn't find it today.

11. The union submitted their list of demands.

12. Make sure that (whoever/whomever) you hire will fix the roof quick.

13. If Danny was taller, he would try out for the basketball team.

14. I support (Ella/Ella's) getting the award — she earned it!

15. Rupert laid awake until three a.m. worrying about his job interview.

16. This is the neighbor on (who/whom) I depend on in emergencies.

17. Toronto is not as far from Chicago as Montreal.

18. I appreciate you watering my plants while I'm gone.

19. (Who/Whom) should I say is calling?

20. The defense mounted by Simpson's lawyers were unbeatable.

21. The crew boss hired (whoever/whomever) was available.

22. Romeo tells Juliet that neither the moon nor the stars is as brilliant as her eyes.

23. All fifteen students know about the quiz but none are studying for it.

24. For (who/whom) do you work?

25. There are no secrets between you and (I/me).

26. Malika felt badly that she was the only one at the party that didn't bring a gift.

27. The Gas Company fired it's chief spokesperson after the power failure last summer.

28. Southwestern State has more recreational facilities than any university in the area.

29. Stephen King is a writer that has had many of his novels made into films.

30. After reading all of her novels, Jane Austen became my favorite author.

31. None of the economic experts agrees.

32. The tollway bill that the governor proposed has no chance of passing.

33. We will either go to the Grand Canyon or to Yosemite.

34. The Bush-Gore presidential race was the first to be mediated by the Supreme Court in 2000.

USAGE/AP STYLE TEST

Correct the following sentences for usage and AP style; most contain multiple errors. If a sentence is correct as is, mark it "OK." *Key on p. 91.*

1. The exhibit is comprised of 100 paintings.

2. I anticipate that the panel will refute my theory when I defend my dissertation.

3. The judge said her pro-life views did not influence her ruling.

4. Over 200 illegal immigrants were killed by drunk drivers last year.

5. The three-member Committee includes Jim, Jane and John.

6. Brian's uncle died suddenly due to a stroke, the doctor claimed.

7. The State Dept. spokesperson would comment no farther.

8. The Cubs' record did not effect their fans' loyalty.

9. Max is anxious about whether he will be able to convince Judy to marry him.

10. You'll make less mistakes if you take a couple minutes to review your answers.

11. Betsy's past experience makes her the number one candidate for the position.

12. Lorelei was so anxious to get the job that she was chomping at the bit for the interview to begin.

13. When she called yesterday, Annie inferred that she collided with the parked car due to the fact that she had been talking on her cell phone while driving.

14. Police said the victim had been strangled to death, but the coroner refused comment before the autopsy was completed.

15. My father lost his extremely unique pocket watch when a fire completely destroyed our house.

16. Rodrigo said that it's not comfortable for him to compare his test score to his roommate.

FINAL LANGUAGE-SKILLS TEST

- Edit to correct errors of punctuation, grammar, usage and AP style.
- Many sentences contain more than one error.
- If a sentence is correct as is, mark it "OK."
- When making word substitutions, retain original meaning, tone and emphasis.
- **Do not change** verb tenses (unless there is a grammatical error) or context!
- *Key on p. 92.*

1. Eddie lie awake with indigestion after eating pizza with hot peppers.

2. Acme, Inc., is one of those companies that has increased the number of its part time employees.

3. None of the negotiators agree.

4. Becky's project is as creative or more creative then her cousin.

5. The string quartet includes two violins, a viola and a harp.

6. Leila suggested whom my choice for council president should be.

7. In his e-mail Bob inferred that he will apply for the position in Baltimore.

8. Nelligan was arrested on charges of strangling his neighbor to death.

9. Whom would you say is the best woman for the job?

10. Between you and I, he knows more sports trivia then me.

11. My nephew's fashion sense is truly unique.

12. The pro-life activists wanted the school nurse fired because of her pro-abortion stance.

13. The law students were chomping at the bit for their bar-exam results.

14. When Marisol was 15 she emigrated to the United States.

15. I appreciate Judy editing my paper — that really made it better.

16. Mary's opinion about the death penalty is different than Tom's.

17. The museum's modern-art collection is comprised of 30 paintings and 20 sculptures.

18. I asked Noni to buy a couple extra bags of chips for the party.

19. "Your pleading will not effect the outcome," the judge said. "Its up to the jury to decide."

20. I wouldn't presume to compare my writing with Shakespeare's, but I would compare it with yours.

21. O'Donnell is the politician who most Illinois voters admire.

22. When it closed last month, the store's inventory was liquidated.

23. Undeterred by a string of recent setbacks that include a car accident, Helen is meeting her deadlines in a way which her boss admires.

24. This is the kitten who climbed up the tree in my back yard.

25. The moving van collided with the garage.

26. The aroma of the grilling steaks mingle with the smell of roasted corn.

27. Jerome could edit faster than anyone in his lab.

28. Harry's grandmother died suddenly.

29. Angie feels badly that she wasn't invited.

30. Reggie lay his keys on the table an hour ago but now he cannot find it.

31. The Red Sox manager congratulated everyone for playing their best.

32. If Bashar was taking less classes he would volunteer more.

33. Michael Jordan is one of those athletes who have carved a place for himself in sports history.

34. None of these dresses are appropriate to wear to the wedding.

35. The paper which I worked on all night is due tomorrow.

36. Hopefully I'll be able to take a break soon.

37. The explosion completely destroyed the building.

38. The nanny told the boy to lay down.

39. Over two million people in the U.S., Europe, and Asia protested the war.

40. All of the Writers' Guild members went on strike, but none was sure the union would win.

41. The editor said: "There are three things I cannot stand; Misspellings, sloppy punctuation, and buried leads."

42. Disaster was avoided due to Meredith's quick thinking.

43. Roxanne is as talented as Jennifer, but not as well known as her.

44. Neither french fries nor potato chips is permitted on your diet.

45. The doctors anticipated that Henry's recovery would be difficult.

46. I was convinced to vote for Yamamoto after he convinced me that he was right on the issues.

47. The candidate refused comment on her opponent's marital problems, and she quickly changed the subject.

48. The firm is considering changing their location.

49. After the five hour meeting, Sanjay was anxious to eat lunch.

50. None of the parties agree to the proposal.

51. Second and third rate films won't make the cut at the Chicago Film Festival.

52. The defense rebutted the prosecution's argument, and the defendant was acquitted.

53. Here's a better idea, I'll order the pizza and you pick it up.

54. Errol lost his wallet, which made him angry.

55. Bonnie asked whom I thought the graduation speaker would be.

Quality-Control Guide to Writing and Editing

Accuracy and Fact-Checking

Accuracy is the basis of journalistic integrity. When the facts aren't right, credibility is in doubt. Common types of factual errors include:

- Spelling of proper nouns (names of people, places, organizations)
- Dates
- Numbers (ages, percentages, dimensions, distances)
- Characterizations (historical, cultural, political)

How to Minimize Factual Errors

Fact-checking should start with the reporting process and continue through the editing process. It is the responsibility of reporters and editors alike.

When reporting and writing:

- Ask sources to repeat and confirm factual references (such as spellings, ages and dates) during interviews
- If something a source said seems unclear in notes or recording of the interview, follow up with the source to clarify
- Double-check facts by consulting other live or published sources when writing the story

When editing:

- Flag facts including proper names, dates and numbers during first read of the story
- Check/correct flagged facts individually after the first read, then do a second read all the way through

When writing and editing, watch out for typos (especially transposed letters and numbers) and don't depend on spell check.

Sources for Fact-Checking

Journalists used to rely on printed reference sources including dictionaries, almanacs and telephone directories. Today these sources and many others are accessible online. Writers and editors must weigh the credibility of online sources and often consult and compare more than one on a given topic. Use Google (and other search engines) to find sources.

- **Primary sources** are original materials generated in the time period to which they refer and have not been interpreted, evaluated or otherwise filtered. These include government documents, speeches, and audio and video recordings.
- **Secondary sources** are usually accounts written after the fact that interpret and evaluate primary sources; media reports can be included in this category.
- **Tertiary sources** distill and collect information. These include almanacs, directories and fact books.

Wiki sources such as Wikipedia and IMDb can be used as guides but are not considered definitive because content is user-generated.

Some reference sources, including *The Associated Press Stylebook*, are accessible online for a fee. There are many free online dictionaries and thesauruses.

FACT-CHECKING EXERCISE

Find and correct the factual and AP style errors. *Key on p. 94.*

1. In his speech, Howe stressed the significance of religion in American thought in the 19th century. He noted that when the transatlantic cable was first laid in 1885, Queen Victoria and President Buchannan exchanged the first message with a Biblical quotation.

2. A little boy collapses on a wide wooden bench.
   "Don't you want to see the Suerat?" his mother asks.
   "I want to sit down," he says.
   Shaking her head, she turns to ponder the painting. Some stare at the work through the lenses of their phones, the magnitude of "A Sunday Afternoon on the Island Park of Le Grande Jette" captured on a screen no bigger than the palm of a hand.

3. The city of Oakville employee daycare budget will increase 54 percent next fiscal year, Mayor Emily Harakawa announced on Monday. Effective July 1, the budget will increase by $636 to $12,270 from $11,637, she said.

4. In July 2013 Illinois became the last state in the U.S. to draft a conceal carry act, after a federal appeals court ruled it unconstitutional for the state to continue its ban on concealed weapons. This act legally enables citizens to carry some types of concealed weapons, heightening concerns of proponents for easing gun restrictions.

5. SEOUL, North Korea — The rival Koreas agreed Wednesday to hold their first reunions of Korean War-divided families in more than three years later this month, another small step to ease tensions despite North Korea's anger over upcoming U.S.-South Koran military drills.

Brevity and Tightening

Brevity is a virtue in journalistic writing. It doesn't require all sentences to be short or to contain mostly one- and two-syllable words. Brevity entails crafting sentences and paragraphs that are streamlined yet sufficiently detailed to be meaningful and clear. Key to achieving this are word economy — in particular averting repetition — and revision, as the following examples show.

A shark-attack story begins with redundant references to water, critical condition and severe injuries connected to a severed leg and the event being unexpected:

> Original: Florida officials are warning beachgoers to exercise caution in the water after a 16-year-old lost a leg and was left in critical condition after sustaining severe injuries in an unexpected shark attack on Monday in Tampa Bay. (37 words)
>
> Revised: Florida officials are warning beachgoers to exercise caution after a 16-year-old lost a leg in a shark attack Monday in Tampa Bay. (22 words)

A brief about a delivery-truck theft contains double references and wordiness:

> Original: When Krispy Kreme deliveryman John Johnson made an early-morning delivery at a White Hen convenience store, he left the engine running on his Krispy Kreme truck and its doors open. (30 words)
>
> Revised: When Krispy Kreme driver John Johnson made an early-morning delivery at a White Hen store, he left the engine running and the truck doors open. (25 words)

A description of a theater performance makes five references to the show in a single paragraph, among other verbosity.

> Original: "Nightmares on Main Street" is the sixth installment of a yearly Halloween performance put on by Veritas Productions. The show incorporates scenes from famous horror films along with several original skits throughout the performance. The cast is comprised of several core actors of Veritas Productions and local talent from open auditions for the show. (54 words)
>
> Revised: "Nightmares on Main Street" is Veritas Productions' sixth annual Halloween show. It incorporates scenes from famous horror films with several original skits. The cast comprises Veritas actors and local talent from open auditions. (33 words)

Good writing is seldom created on first pass but rather is the result of revision. Get the idea down first, then go back to trim the fat and polish the prose.

Original: Listening to people's conversations reveals the true brilliance of those in Tech. Mentions of polymers or chemical volatility tell a story of the knowledge contained in the minds of those who either teach or learn within the building. One might think that between all the people occupying the many offices and all the students learning in the classrooms, one could find all the knowledge in the world. (67 words)

Revised: Conversations at Tech reverberate with esoteric details of polymers and chemical volatility, among other things. It would seem that here — in offices, classrooms and labs — the keys to all the knowledge in the world can be found. (37 words)

Original: It is easy to lose track of time at Chai House, spending hours enjoying multiple beverages and getting work done. A couple passes by on Sherman Avenue with a black and silver blanket shrouding a stroller, with a young boy's head peeking out of the front through the fur of his coat hood. This serves as a reminder for the cold that awaits beyond the warmth the teashop offers on a brisk winter afternoon. (74 words)

Revised: It is easy to lose track of time at Chai House sipping one cup after another while working or observing the world outside. A couple wheels by on Sherman Avenue, a stroller shrouded by a black-and-silver blanket. The young passenger peeks through his fur hood — a reminder of the winter beyond the warmth of the teashop. (56 words)

TIGHTENING EXERCISE

Edit the following to the target word counts. *Key on p. 95.*

1. Attorney and women's rights activist Rondi Vega is scheduled to speak on March 27 at Southeastern University about the need for women to speak up about issues important to them in this year's women's leadership lecture. (36 words; trim to 18)

2. Many students at universities in the United States have expressed support for President Obama's views regarding marijuana usage, which were published in an interview in this week's issue of The New Yorker magazine. (33 words; trim to 21)

3. During his lecture, Grantham discussed the means by which ideas are spread through the medium of social networks. (18 words; trim to 9)

4. As hundreds of incoming college students gathered on Greening Meadow in the middle of September, the Arcadia University campus and setting sun set the perfect atmosphere. Among the freshmen one stood tall above the rest. (35 words; trim to 23)

5. Commuters are finding it impossible to escape the extreme cold that is pounding the Midwest — not even the "Frostbite Express" shuttle service titled after the weather is enough to provide escape from the chills. (34 words; trim to 21)

6. An unidentified man was found dead Wednesday night after his body was discovered on the front porch of a Fernwood residence after a shooting in Oakdale, said police, who do not have witnesses in the case or know how many shots were fired. (43 words; trim to 19)

Clarity

In Quotations

Issues of clarity can arise in quotes. On first reference, identify a person by full name and title or a specific appositive phrase. In the following example, assume Miller has already been identified and note boldface insertions to clarify: bracketed content within the quote and an appositive phrase outside it.

> "One of the valuable things about a nuclear deal with Iran," Miller said, "is that it could empower moderates such as **[Iranian President Hassan]** Rouhani.
>
> "Who will define Iran in the coming generations? Is it going to be people like Ahmadinejad, who seem to take pride and pleasure in confronting the West," **Miller said, referring to Rouhani's controversial predecessor.** "Or will it be defined by people like Rouhani and his foreign minister, **[Javad]** Zarif, who prefer diplomacy?"

Avoid bumping or stacking quotes back to back. Insert a transition between quotes to clarify where one ends and the next begins.

> Lee's background was a major factor in her decision to seek the position of Southwest University's first director of inclusion. "My work is to help people define themselves so they can find their own spaces in the community," she said. "I do that every day."
>
> "Identity issues were a big part of our undergraduate experience," said Leta Chan, Lee's former roommate at Sylvan College. "We navigated them all the time. She will likely channel that personal experience in her new post at Southwest."
>
> Revise second graf: Lee is likely to channel her personal experience in her new post at Southwest. "Identity issues were a big part of our undergraduate experience," said Leta Chan, Lee's former roommate at Sylvan College. "We navigated them all the time."

Time Elements

Misplaced time elements can also obscure clarity.

> Not: A body has been found near a popular fishing spot on the Calumet River for the second time this winter.
>
> But: A body has been found near a popular fishing spot on the Calumet River, the second such discovery this winter.

> Not: For the second time in three years, the Topeka City Council voted Monday to increase parking meter fees by 15 percent, raising the price to $1.15 an hour.
>
> But: The Topeka City Council voted Monday to increase parking meter fees by 15 percent to $1.15 an hour, the second hike in three years.

Getting Details Right

Too much detail upfront can hinder clarity. Scale back in the lead and indicate secondary details later:

> Not: A 37-year-old man and a 34-year-old woman found dead in a house in the 1500 block of Honeysuckle Lane at 6:22 a.m. on Wednesday are thought by police to have died in a murder-suicide.
>
> But: A man and woman found dead in a house on Honeysuckle Lane Wednesday morning may have died in a murder-suicide, police said.

Detail used in the right proportion can clarify relativity, scope and venue:

> A teenage girl died of a shark attack last week.
>
> *A 14-year-old girl died of a shark attack in Florida last week, the ninth in the state so far this year.*
>
> The girl's younger brother Andrew described the attack.
>
> *The girl's brother Andrew, 12, described the attack, which he witnessed from the beach.*

When further detail is needed for clarification but **can't be assumed**, <u>ask</u>. What details missing from the following paragraphs should the writer supply?

> Vera Robbins, 24, who has been working at FroYo Delight for the last three years, says the market for professional jobs is tight. "People can find jobs if they're not picky about what's available," she said. "It's harder for people who have college degrees and are overqualified."
>
> Michael Tanaka, 36, took a job in a grocery store last month rather than be unemployed. But the pay is less than what he earned in his last job, and the work is below his qualifications. "They want to start you at the bottom and work your way up no matter what your experience is," he said.

- Does Vera have a college degree? If so, in what field?
- What was Michael's last job? How much of a pay cut did he take to work at the grocery store?

CLARITY EXERCISE

Identify missing details in each paragraph that would clarify the following story. *Key on p. 96.*

According to the U.S. Bureau of Labor Statistics, unemployment among 16-year-olds and over has dropped by 1.3 percent over the past year. Similarly, unemployment among young adults ages 25 and over has declined by 1.1 percent. (**P1**)

Despite these gains, workers and students in Evansville say the employment landscape remains challenging. Betsy Marks, 26, manager of the MetaMe boutique, is staying in her job despite other career goals. "I'm constantly updating my resume and looking at what would I be interested in if I wasn't working here," she said. (**P2**)

Six years after graduating from college, Sammy Washington, 28, said he does not have a clear path to a career. "I've noticed fewer layoffs but not more opportunities," he said. (**P3**)

Evansville College sophomore Mary Dodd, 19, says the structure of the job market has an impact on the availability of jobs. "There's an educated working class that's facing widespread underemployment because people expect to attain higher-level jobs than they currently have," said Dodd, who works part time as a restaurant server in order to improve her resume and customer-service skills. (**P4**)

"More people should study crafts and trades to be qualified for those types of jobs, which are in greater supply," said senior Mark Clark, 21. Still, he said he is confident that earning a college degree will ensure him a prestigious professional job. (**P5**)

Quotations and Attribution

Quotations in stories have three important functions:

- They impart authority, indicating the source/s of information
- They put readers in touch with the subject/s of the story, making it relatable and easier to understand
- They make the story more interesting, adding voice, tone and color

Change Quote Content with Care

Use quotation marks to indicate the speaker's exact words. Do not make up quotes or assume that a statement not in quotes is a direct quote — ask when in doubt. Make changes to the content of direct quotes carefully, always preserving context. Rules on how and whether quotes can be changed vary from classroom to classroom and newsroom to newsroom — so know what is permitted where you are working.

In general, one-word grammar fixes and one- or two-word insertions to enhance clarity are allowed *if* doing so will not take the speaker's words out of context. Edited quotes should *never* change the speaker's intended meaning or emphasis.

Make a one-word grammar fix unless doing so would change the speaker's tone. (For example, if the dialect uses "setting" to mean "sitting," leave it as is.)

> Original: "This breakthrough is an exciting phenomena," Jones said.
>
> Edited: "This breakthrough is an exciting phenomenon," Jones said.
>
> Or paraphrase: Jones said the breakthrough is an exciting phenomenon.

Insert one or two bracketed words for clarity if the context doesn't provide it:

> Original: "I will accept the cut," Reed said, "but I am not happy about it."
>
> Edited: "I will accept the [salary] cut," Reed said, "but I am not happy about it."

When to Paraphrase

Not everything a source says is quote-worthy:

> Coach Pat Jones said: "This team is the strongest it has been in decades. Our recruiting has paid off, and our defense is unbeatable."

Don't paraphrase everything and omit direct quotation altogether:

> Coach Pat Jones said the team is stronger than it has been in decades, recruiting has paid off and the defense is unbeatable.

Find the right balance between direct quotation and paraphrasing:

> According to coach Pat Jones, the team is stronger than it has been in decades. "Our recruiting has paid off, and our defense is unbeatable," she said.

If a quote is weak, paraphrase it:

> Original: "We're grateful no one was injured, no property was damaged and that the elephants are fine," zookeeper Sally O'Reilly said.
>
> Edited: There were no injuries or property damage, and the elephants are fine, a zoo official said.

Eliminate redundancy between lead-in and quote, paraphrasing where appropriate:

> Original: Lopez said she will visit India next summer. "I will travel there on my summer break," she said.
>
> Edited: Lopez said she will travel to India next summer.
>
> Original: The village board said raising taxes is the only way to fund road improvement. "There is no other way to pay for it," trustee Leila Abdul said.
>
> Edited: The village board stood by its decision to raise taxes for road improvement. "There is no other way to pay for it," trustee Leila Abdul said.

If a quote is libelous, delete it and paraphrase where appropriate:

> Original: "I knew something suspicious was going on next door," Richards said. "People were always coming and going late at night. They must have been dealing drugs."
>
> Edited: Richards said he often saw people going in and out of his next-door neighbor's house late at night.

Shorten Quotes for Brevity, Impact and Fairness

If a quote runs long (generally more than two sentences), tighten it:

> Original: "I couldn't believe my eyes at first," Parker said. "It was the middle of the night, it was dark and I was tired, so I thought maybe my imagination was playing tricks on me. But it's pretty difficult to mistake an elephant for anything else."
>
> Edited: "I thought my imagination was playing tricks on me," Parker said. "But it's difficult to mistake an elephant for anything else."

If a quote includes phrases denoting feelings or emotions that do not advance an essential idea, delete them:

> Original: "I really think that the ruling was unfair," Chin said.
>
> Edited: "The ruling was unfair," Chin said.

But don't edit out elements that add emphasis or context:

> "There is no doubt that the court made a grave error," Chin said.

If only part of the quote "sings," use a partial quote (also called a snippet):

> Original: "I disagree with this policy, which is discriminatory and will result in lawsuits," Stein said.
>
> Edited: Stein disagreed with the policy, saying it "is discriminatory and will result in lawsuits."

Running Quotations and Ellipses

If a quote continues from one paragraph to the next, don't use close-quote marks at the end of the first paragraph. Use open-quote marks at the start of the second paragraph and close-quote marks at the end of the quoted material.

> "The unemployment rate has had many severe impacts," the state comptroller said, "including reductions in income tax and sales tax revenues.
>
> "This will result in education, entitlement and social service cutbacks."

(See AP stylebook for further guidelines for when a paragraph does not begin with a quote or ends in a partial quote.)

In general, ellipses aren't needed to indicate shortening of ordinary spoken quotations. Use ellipses to indicate omissions in citation of published texts such as speech transcripts and literary works. Again, take care not to present quoted material out of its original context.

Use Attribution Properly

For simple attribution, the preferred order is *subject-verb*:

> Not: "The festival will be even bigger this year," said Smith.
> But: "The festival will be even bigger this year," Smith said.

For attribution that includes an appositive or descriptive phrase, the preferred order is *verb-subject*:

> "The festival will be even bigger this year," said Smith, who was appointed director last year.

In a single-sentence quote, attribution usually works best at the end:

"We will overcome our economic difficulties and emerge even stronger than before," the president said.

Use general attribution and paraphrasing in most summary news leads, followed by direct quotes with specific attribution:

The Corps of Engineers expects the snow that has blanketed the Midwest in recent weeks to be of little help in solving the low-water crisis on the Mississippi River.

"The good news is that the river is still open," corps spokesman Mike Petersen said. "But it will take a lot more snow to get us out of the danger zone."

In a multisentence quote, place attribution at the first logical break:

"We will overcome our economic difficulties and emerge even stronger than before," the president said. "These new policies will stimulate investment and create jobs."

Original: "My business was hurt the last time parking fees were raised. If people have to pay more to park, they'll spend less at Hot Dog Hut," Janet Cooper, owner of Hot Dog Hut said.

Edited: "My business was hurt the last time parking fees were raised," said Hot Dog Hut owner Janet Cooper. "If people have to pay more to park, they'll spend less."

Use full-name and title attribution on first reference, last name on second and subsequent references. Alternate name and pronoun use:

Gov. Rena Reilly said she will not run for re-election next year and has accepted an academic position at State University.

Reilly said she wants to spend more time with her family. "I need to step back from public life and focus on other things," she said.

Attribute plans, expectations, feelings and beliefs rather than stating them as facts:

Original: The coroner will perform the autopsy on Tuesday and identify the body by the end of the week.

Edited: The coroner said she will perform an autopsy on Tuesday and expects to identify the body by the end of the week.

Not: Lipinski is excited about her new job.

But: Lipinski said she is excited about her new job.

Not: Roberts doesn't believe the bill will pass.

But: Roberts said he doesn't believe the bill will pass.

Use neutral verbs for attribution (e.g., said, stated) rather than terms that imply agreement (e.g., explained, revealed, pointed out) unless the context supports it. Avoid terms that imply guilt (e.g., admitted, claimed) unless the context supports it.

Not: Jarvis pointed out that climate change is a myth.

But: Jarvis said climate change is a myth.

Not: The physics professor stated the theory of relativity.

But: The physics professor explained the theory of relativity.

Not: Bob admitted he is gay.

But: Bob said he is gay.

Not: The boy claimed that he didn't take his classmate's bicycle.

But: The boy said he didn't take his classmate's bicycle.

QUOTATIONS AND ATTRIBUTION EXERCISE

Edit the following based on the guidelines above. *Key on p. 96.*

1. Jesse Brown has been a newspaper editor for 30 years but explains that technology has not changed many of the basics.

   "Many of the fundamentals have not changed," Jesse Brown said. "Journalists still have to exercise news judgment, cultivate sources and use language clearly. And most important, I really think that they need to be ethical in their reporting methods and balanced in their presentation."

   "These common denominators doesn't change, no matter what new technologies enable us to do," said Brown.

2. "I started researching my family history 15 years ago," 85-year-old Jane Findlay said. "I started at zero. I knew about nothing before my grandparents' generation. I really didn't know what to do, but the more I found out, the more fascinating it became.

   Findlay said she thinks it's important to keep her family history alive. "I will continue to research the family history for as long as I can," Findlay said. "This is my gift to my grandchildren and to their children one day."

3. Gov.-elect Royce Brauner said on Tuesday that "the time has come for a change in the way we do business in this state. My administration will no longer do business as usual with regard to costly programs and labor practices we can no longer afford."

   "I will affect change in every way I know how," Gov. Brauner said, including cutting ineffective and costly programs while using new ways to attract business to the state.

Basic Editing Principles

Editing is a collaborative process. Editors should consult with writers before making substantive changes whenever possible to avert incorrect assumptions leading to introduced errors.

1. Accuracy, Brevity and Clarity

These are the hallmarks of well-edited copy. By fact-checking, editors make the text *accurate*; by tightening, they make it *brief* and *succinct*; and by rewording, restructuring and patching holes, they make it *clear*.

Well-edited copy answers all questions it raises, both explicitly and implicitly, and it presents a logical flow of information and ideas. Facts and spellings must be correct, numbers must add up and sources must be properly attributed.

2. Editing vs. Rewriting

Editors draw on a number of skills to improve the text, but they do not write it. The editor must respect the writer's voice and resist the temptation to rewrite based on the idea that *"If I were writing this, here's how it would read."*

Rewriting should be done sparingly unless the copy is unclear, wordy or otherwise problematic. Edits should be as unobtrusive as possible and maintain the writer's original tone and emphasis.

3. If It Ain't Broke . . .

Some types of edits are objective, including fact, grammar and spelling fixes. Other types of edits are subjective and should be made judiciously. As the saying goes: *If it ain't broke, don't fix it!* Subjective edits should improve copy by making it clearer and more succinct. Editors should double-check their work to avert introducing error.

4. Skill Integration

Skilled editors work on three levels at once: *mechanical, structural* and *conceptual.* Mechanical edits correct errors of spelling, grammar, punctuation, word usage, syntax and style. The editor's mastery of language skills and style should necessitate only infrequent consulting of reference sources on these points. Structural edits improve organization, brevity, transitions and flow. Conceptual edits address accuracy, clarity and completeness by fact-checking and rewording in consultation with the writer.

5. The Ethos of Editing

In Arabic the noun *tahrir* has two meanings: *liberation* and *editing.* The active participles, *muharrir* (masc.) and *muharrira* (fem.), can mean either *liberator* or *editor.* These related meanings give us the idea that editors liberate copy, freeing it from error, ambiguity and other shortcomings.

Answer Keys

1. Professor Nelson began the lecture and passed out a quiz. (**OK**)

2. Professor Nelson began the **lecture but** did not call on me.

3. Professor Nelson gave a long **lecture, but** he did not use any notes.

4. Professor Nelson began the lecture and he immediately captured our attention. (**OK**)

5. My grandfather was **re-elected** to a fifth term as the mayor of Hometown, **Illinois,** on April 1, **2010,** in a landslide victory.

6. They **met,** they **dated,** they broke up.

7. Here today, gone tomorrow. (**OK**)

8. She is survived by a sister, Rachel. (**OK**)

9. He is survived by his wife, Rhonda; two sons, Jules and **Jim;** and a grandchild, George.

10. I love epic films, especially the Oscar-winning best **picture "Titanic."**

11. It was **unbelievable: The** Wildcats pulled off another last-minute victory!

    or: It was **unbelievable** — **the** Wildcats pulled off another last-minute victory!

    It was **unbelievable that** the Wildcats pulled off another last-minute victory.

12. "When will the new budget be **ready?"** the alderman asked the mayor.

13. "This budget will never be **passed,"** the alderman said. "Can you revise it?"

14. "Now this," the alderman **said, "is** a much more realistic budget."

15. The mayor called his finance officer **"brilliant."**

16. The mayor **said, "Listen,** colleagues, we've got to work together."

17. **This year** the Board of Education averted a **teachers** strike.

18. June chose white, **pink** and yellow roses for her bridal bouquet.

19. Jerry served salad, garlic **bread,** and spaghetti and meatballs for dinner.

20. He saw the car, he wanted the **car** and he bought the car.

21. I like anchovy **pizza;** most of my friends cannot stand it.

22. My **old,** two-story house is expensive to heat.

23. The parka was filled with soft goose down. **(OK)**

24. Observing the passengers on the train, she **said,** gave her an idea for a short story.

25. Because Robert snores his wife can't get any sleep. **(OK)**

26. Because his snoring keeps her **awake,** Robert and his wife sleep in separate rooms.

27. My car, which was **well-maintained,** lasted 10 years.

28. **People** who live in glass **houses** buy a lot of Windex.

29. The president has a **five-year** plan for **health care** reform.
*(AP style: **Health care** is not hyphenated as an adjective.)*

30. The **26-year-old** man was the youngest CEO in the industry.

31. When it came to discipline, the coach treated his **first-** and **second-string** players alike.

32. Modernizing the stadium is a **multimillion-dollar** project.

33. Jamila likes taking long walks. **But** she likes them less in cold weather.

or: Jamila likes taking long **walks, but** she likes them less in cold weather.

34. Bill gave his best **friend, Al,** some tips on fundraising.

35. Lucy gave her friend Ethel a headache. **(OK)**

36. The dean **said:** "This is the best freshman class we have had in a long time. They did especially well in editing."

37. The bigamist's wife Jan was upset with her husband's other **wife, Suzie,** and Suzie's only **brother,** Tim.

38. After the lumberjack sawed his last **log,** cabin fever overcame him.

GRAMMAR TERMS AND CONCEPTS EXERCISE

I. **Identify the parts of speech *for each word* in the sentences below.**

Use the abbreviations indicated in parentheses for these choices:

noun (**N**) article (**art**) adjective (**adj**)
pronoun (**pro**) preposition (**prep**) adverb (**adv**)
verb/infinitive verb (**V/inf V**) conjunction (**conj**) interjection (**int**)

    N   V   art   N   prep art   N   conj pro   V
1. John threw the book across the room, and they gasped.

     adj   N   V adj   inf V conj pro V adj
2. Foreign languages are easy to learn when one is young.

     int inf V prep N   V pro   adj   N
3. Yes, to live in France is my wildest dream.

    N V art pro pro   V pro art N
4. Ellie is the one who gave me the gift.

II. **Find the grammatical functions *of the italicized words* in the sentences below.**

Use the abbreviations indicated in parentheses for these choices:

subject (**S**) direct object (**DO**) predicate nominative (**PN**)
predicate (**P**) indirect object (**IO**) predicate adjective (**PA**)
                object of preposition (**OP**)

   S   P   DO   OP   S   P
1. *John threw* the *book* across the *room*, and *they gasped.*

         S   P PA   S P PA
2. Foreign *languages are easy* to learn when *one is young.*

      S   P   PN
3. Yes, *to live* in France *is* my wildest *dream.*

    S P   PN   S   P   IO   DO
4. *Ellie is* the *one who gave me* the *gift.*

III. **Decline these personal pronouns according to case:**

nominative	I	you	he	she	it	we	they	who/whoever
objective	me	you	him	her	it	us	them	whom/whomever
possessive	my	your	his	her	its	our	their	whose
	mine	yours		hers		ours	theirs	

GRAMMAR SELF-TEST I

$$$$

             S   V

1. [This is the man] **who** lives next door.

   S   V   PN

2. **Who** was the first man on the moon?

                        S   V

3. [The committee believed] **her** to be the best choice.
(subject of infinitive verb takes objective case)

                     DO   S   V

4. [The police knew] **whom** they would question first.

                S   V

5. [I was asked] **who** [I thought] would win the race.

                             PN   S   V

6. [The reporter was determined not to tell] **who** her source was.

                     S   V

7. [Priyanka is the writer] **who** will be nominated for the award.

                     S   V

8. [The reporter interviewed] **whoever** would talk on the record.

                     prep OP/DO   S   V

9. [The photographer works] with **whomever** the agency recommends.

10. If I **were** French, I could translate the novel easily. *(subjunctive)*

                    DO   S   V

11. [Anderson was the candidate] **whom** the Independent Party chose.

12. I appreciate **you** giving the workers time off — what a generous employer! *(emphasis on person)*

13. Streep is one of those **actors who are** able to do accents well.

        S   V

14. **Who** [will I know] is the right man?

  prep OP

15. To **whom** should I address my question?

16. Jay is a craftsman **who** takes pride in getting the details right.

17. I am not **so** patient as you are. *(negative comparison)*

18. I believe that **your** repaying the loan will improve our relationship. *(emphasis on action)*

19. These are the pandas **that** the zoo recently acquired.

                  prep   OP

20. There are no secrets between you and **me**.

GRAMMAR SELF-TEST II

1. A number of reporters **were** assigned to cover the convention.

2. He worked at a slower pace than anyone **else** in the class.

   or: He worked at **the slowest** pace **of** anyone in the class.

3. I feel **bad** for him.

4. The building has 50 offices, and all **except** one have gray carpet. The one **that** is the biggest is the president's office. The business **office, which has no windows,** is the smallest.

   or: ... The president's office is the biggest. ...

5. The defense of Tinker, Evers and Chance **is** unbeatable.

6. Smith told Jones **he** would paint **his** car. (*ambiguous*)

7. None of the parties agrees to this proposal. (**OK**)

8. Either the dogs or the cat is bound to run away. (**OK**)

9. Ariel **lay** down to take a nap but slept until the next morning.

10. The BP oil spill was **a** historic event.

11. The students applauded their teachers and recalled **their** best moments in the classroom. (*ambiguous*)

12. None of our tax returns **has** been audited.

13. The computers **that** you will find here have the latest operating system.

    or: The **computers you** will find here have the latest operating system.

    The **computers, which you will find here,** have the latest operating system.

14. Olga likes to skate better **than I.**

15. I **laid** my keys on the table yesterday; today I cannot find **them.**

16. Although **his** calendar was full, **the lawyer** made time for pro bono clients.

    or: Although **he had a full calendar**, the lawyer ...

17. Jonas **will accept not only** his award but **also** my award.

18. None of the parties to the conflict **agree.**

19. We **will vacation either** in Hawaii or in Acapulco.

20. The team played without discipline, **and that** bothered the coach.

    or: The team played without discipline, **bothering** the coach.

    The **team's playing without discipline** bothered the coach.

    The coach **was bothered because** the team played without discipline.

21. All 15 pilots attended the seminar, but none was enthusiastic about it. (**OK**)

22. The police officers told **them all/all of them** to lay their weapons down.

23. **I saw the tall trees bending in the breeze**.

24. The academy submitted **its** list of candidates.

25. **In 2011** Etta Jones **became** the first woman to be elected mayor of Manleyville.

USAGE SELF-TEST

1. **Jones'** approach is different **from** his wife's.

2. The Norrises' neighbor was found **strangled**.

3. We did not **expect** that the club would sell **its** membership list to telemarketers.

4. Jimmy could not **persuade** the car dealer to ignore his credit report, **his wife said**.

5. His approach to the problem is **unique**.

6. If I had **fewer** problems, I would be less depressed.

7. The CEO died **unexpectedly** without having named a successor.

8. The fire **destroyed** the house, which was worth **approximately/an estimated** $300,000.

9. The president **declined to** comment **only** on the plan to invade Tobago.

10. I compared my test results **with** my **roommate's**.

11. Nine blacks, two whites and a Latino **composed/made up** the jury.

    or: The **jury comprised** nine blacks, two whites and a Latino.

12. From what you said, I **inferred** that you'll come to my party.

13. Charlotte **implied discreetly** that she would run for the school board.

14. Roger vowed to run as fast **as** or faster **than** his rival.

15. A couple **of** more laps and you will be finished with practice.

16. The class was postponed for over a week **because of** the teacher's illness.

17. I have traveled **farther** than you but have visited **fewer** countries.

18. Walid **said** he had never met the man.

19. The student driver **hit/ran into/crashed into** the stop sign.

20. The candidate **continually rebutted** her opponent's charges.

21. After not eating for seven hours, Jerry was **eager** to have dinner.

22. The food pantry **disbursed an abundance** of canned goods to the city's 10,000 homeless.

23. The new administration is **expected** to **effect** change.

24. Your preparation will **affect** your ability to perform well.

25. The first day of school will be **Tuesday in Milwaukee** and **Wednesday in the northern suburbs**.

26. The three suspects **are** a doctor, a lawyer and an accountant.

27. The jurors were **champing** at the bit to reach a verdict so they could go home.

28. Tonya's **experience** abroad has helped her to understand Japanese culture.

    not: Tonya's past abroad has helped her to understand Japanese culture. *(unintended innuendo)*

29. John Lennon compared his music **to** the Gospel.

30. The **pro-abortion-rights** rally was held in front of the White House.

RECAP: COMPREHENSIVE SELF-TEST

1. The candidate vowed to **effect** change in three areas**:** **health** care, the **deficit** and education.

2. Last **year** I was not **so** tall as you, but this year I grew more than 6 inches.

3. My **friend Vinnie** compared his real estate taxes **with** mine.

4. I **shopped,** I **charged,** I **owed;** they billed, they **dunned,** they repossessed.

5. The couple from **Yonkers, New York,** moved to 200 Linden **Drive, Phoenix,** on May **4,** 2010.

6. It was the head nurse **who asked,** "**Who** is responsible for this mix-up?"

7. My oldest **brother,** David, loves to watch old TV shows including "Mission: Impossible," "Hill Street **Blues,**" and "The Sonny **and** Cher Show."

8. If I **were** you, I would not entrust a **multimillion-dollar** project to my brother-in-law.

9. Remember this: **The** couple **were** injured because they weren't wearing seat belts.

10. North America **comprises** three **countries:** Canada, the United **States** and Mexico.

11. We looked at **first-** and **second-floor** apartments in the **building,** which you recommended.

    or: ... building **that** you recommended. *or:* ... **building you** recommended.

12. Roland **said:** "None of the taxes **have★** been paid. The bank will repossess our farm."

13. What I bought Sally for her **birthday,** he said, is not what she **expected**.

14. The actress **refused** to answer **questions** and she shouted at the reporters to leave her alone.

15. **I lost my expensive leather briefcase while traveling in Europe.**

    or: **My expensive leather** briefcase was lost **when I was traveling in Europe**.

16. My new car has a **dent,** which bothers me.

    or: ... a **dent that** bothers me. *or:* ... a dent, **and that** bothers me.

17. The **neighbors** who live to the south of **us** admire our garden.

18. Give **us**, the student body, lower **tuition,** free **parking** and better housing.

19. The gambler **laid** his cards on the table and said, "**Friends,** I have a royal flush."

20. My new car has a CD **player** but not cruise control.

21. "Give the report to **whomever** you want," the mayor's press secretary said.

22. I must object to **him** getting the award, because I deserve it more.

23. The mayor, crushed between her top aides and **me**, began to panic.

24. You're looking **well** — are you over your cold?

25. He wondered **whom** he could ask to look into the matter **further**.

26. If I **were** you, I would demand that your attacker be brought to justice.

27. Pressing their attack, **the media made the mayor their next target**.

28. It is **we** who are the victims.

29. It was **I** you saw at the KitKat Club.

30. If you add a couple **of** dried red peppers, your chili will be as hot **as** or hotter **than** mine.

31. Woody Allen is one of those actors who never **seem** to be at ease on the screen.

32. The president **had only** one **option,** but he described several scenarios.

33. Can you believe that I just **lay** on the beach all summer?

★ *One-word grammar fixes may be permitted in direct quotes. Check specific classroom or newsroom guidelines.*

34. There **go** the best team and best coach in baseball.

35. Nobody studied harder than **I** for this exam.

36. Northwestern will **play either** Illinois or Michigan.

37. Neither the coach nor the team **wants** to do anything that would hurt the university's image.

38. The couple **were** separated for nine hours during the earthquake.

39. I know **whom** you think to be the best candidate.

40. Police frisked **whoever** came through the gate.

41. None of the passengers **was** injured when the train derailed and **crashed into** the mountain.

42. Be careful: I just might be **on to** you.

43. This prosecutor would charge **whoever** walks through that door next if he thought it would advance his career.

44. I agree that **his** storming out of the room aggravated the situation, but it did not start the trouble.

45. There has never been **so** great an estrangement as there is now between Hannah and her sister.

46. It took **a while**, but trust grew **among** the three of us.

47. None of us **goes** out as much as before.

48. Neither of the first-place winners **plans** to donate **her** prize money to charity.

49. Repeated mistakes made the teacher grow **quick** to criticize his students.

50. Just **lay** the book over **there,** and I'll pick it up later.

AP STYLE SELF-TEST I

1. The blizzard hit the Midwest hardest, particularly **northern** Illinois.

2. **Public School 7** raised the price of lunch to **$2.30**.

3. Sasha and wife Svetlana went camping near Jackson Hole, **Wyoming,** this summer. *or:* Sasha and **his** wife**, Svetlana,** ...

4. The suburban law firm moved downtown to 225 **W.** Washington **St.**

5. 1978 was the year John Paul **II** became **pope**.

6. NASA was established as the **U.S.** space agency in the late **1950s**.

7. Derek Johnson reported on **Rep.** Jones until it came out that he had worked for **Jones** as an intern.

8. The **6-foot-11-inch** center was bypassed in the draft for the **5-foot-8-inch** guard.

9. During the trial the defendant asserted **that** he did not kill his wife.

10. The storm dumped 7 inches of rain on the North Shore suburbs.

11. Natural disasters including earthquakes and mudslides have plagued Southern California in recent years. (**OK**)

12. The **First** Amendment has 45 words contained in one paragraph.

13. CHICAGO — A **Boston** man was arrested Tuesday in connection with insider-trading schemes at the **Chicago Board of Trade**.

14. The House voted **300-135** to cut **$60 billion** from the federal budget.

15. The Lakeview **Neighborhood Association** parade route is bounded by Diversey and Belmont **avenues** and Halsted and Clark streets.

16. American foreign policy does not always reflect public opinion in the **U.S.**

17. Fritz ordered **french** fries and a **Manhattan** cocktail.

18. Customs for care of elderly parents in the **East differ** from such customs in the **West**.

19. The White House is located at 1600 Pennsylvania **Ave.**, not far from the offices of **The** Washington Post.

20. "**Dr.** Bond and **Gov.** Cash are ideal candidates for the trade commission," Sen. Steve Stephens said.

21. The Plano, **Texas**, woman won the lottery while visiting her cousin in **Cleveland**.

22. Williams contended **that** her boss owed her two **months'** back pay.

23. Acting **Mayor** Ginger Grant appointed Jonas Grumby **minister** of **transportation**.

24. Ahmad's two **daughters-in-law** were among the **passers-by** injured when the van jumped the curb.

25. I put two **teaspoonfuls** of sugar in my coffee.

26. Jodie's mother and aunt are Yale University **alumnae**.

27. The hurricane destroyed the **children's** hospital and the **teachers** college.

28. The relationship between social media and traditional media has become a popular topic for many **master's theses**.

29. The Christmas song admonishes: Be good for **goodness'** sake.

30. Herbert Bang is a friend of my **father's** and a supporter of the National Rifle **Association**.

31. The **deer's** tracks led to the Marine **Corps'** training camp.

    or: **deer** tracks; **Corps** (*as adjectives*)

32. The Supreme Court is expected to rule at **9 a.m. Monday**.

33. The scissors **are** in my desk drawer.

34. Fourteen **people** attended the creative-writing workshop.

35. The mumps **was** the first childhood disease my sister had.

36. The **peoples** of the Middle East speak many languages, and their countries are represented in the **U.N.**

37. The second **witness's** answer contradicted the first **witness'** story.

38. The property-tax and handgun issues will be voted on in special **referendums**.

39. The **Joneses** live to the south of us.

40. I **really** had to guess at what she meant.

41. Ann's home library includes **Webster's New World Dictionary**, "The Rise **and** Fall of **the** Third Reich" and a worn copy of **the** Bible.

42. **Sgt. Maj.** Lovely commended **Pvts.** Fine and Dandy.

43. Xena usually **had gone** to battle accompanied by Gabrielle.

AP STYLE SELF-TEST II

1. The English **department** offers 20 literature courses each fall.

2. The junior high school principal **on Monday** suspended the girls who played the prank.

or: **On Monday** the junior high school principal ...

3. Mayor Rogers announced **on** Friday **that** Gainesville will make a bid to host the Summer Olympics.

4. The **18-year-old man** was the youngest hired by the **100-year-old** company.

5. The business world was rocked by the merger of First Bank **Ltd.** and United Finance **Corp.**

6. **Mickey Mantle** hit the most home runs in the American League in 1955.

7. I talked to my cousin **on Wednesday** about the **freelance** article I'm writing.

8. The **fundraising** dinner for the new gymnasium was the PTA's **No. 1** priority.

9. Gates was in his **mid-20s** in the **mid-'70s**.

10. The student club's **finance committee** was inspired to do **fundraising** by the Senate **Foreign Relations Committee** vote to send aid to Afghanistan.

11. After serving a 15-year **prison** sentence for armed robbery, Cunningham began working **part time**.

12. **Celebrating Mass** is an important ritual in the Roman Catholic **Church**.

13. **After** her **drunken** driving conviction, **professor** Lori **Evans** began attending Alcoholics Anonymous meetings.

14. The actor's **representative** did not return the reporter's phone calls.

15. The Greenville **City Council** has excellent relations with the **Police Department**.

16. Marcel got a **full-time** job working for the **Department** of Motor Vehicles.

17. In February **Dr.** Lucinda Rodriguez celebrated her **10th** year as a practicing physician.

18. A cure for cancer would benefit all **humanity**.

19. The gay **hotline** has two **full-time** staffers.

20. Monica moved heaven and **earth** to enroll her daughter in the **church child care** program.

AP STYLE SELF-TEST III

1. Some activists still call themselves **Marxists** despite the decline of **communism**.

2. The Commonwealth of Independent States comprises **11 of the** former republics of the **USSR**, with Russia as the largest.

3. Many truck drivers belong to the **Teamsters union**.

4. Sam S. Smith was convicted of murder. (**OK;** retain middle initial)

5. The **Sept. 11** attacks are thought to be the work of **al-Qaida**.

6. Jane spends an hour a day **online** reading and sending **email**.

7. We saw the sites of **Jesus' crucifixion** and **his** believed **resurrection** on a tour of Jerusalem's Old City.

8. Reps. Jan Bowers, **R-Fla.,** and Lan Flowers, **D-Ark.,** co-authored a bipartisan **health care**-reform bill.

9. The Federal Deposit Insurance **Corp.** underwrites some **Public Broadcasting Service** programming.

10. The resignation of the prime minister caused an uproar in the Knesset, Israel's **parliament**.

11. **Bill Clinton** was the first second-term **Democrat** since FDR.

12. Hinckley and Schmidt were among the **reporters/journalists** assigned to cover the **Republican National Convention**.

13. The **U.S. Postal Service** will raise its rates again next year.

14. Ed's first task as **webmaster** is to redesign the company's **website**.

15. Marie's grandparents were married in **January 1950**, and her mother, Amelia, was born on **Feb. 15, 1951**.

16. The headquarters of the **National Organization for Women** is in **Washington, D.C.** *or:* **Washington**.

17. **The** Rev. Joe Martin traveled to Rome and met the **pope**.

18. Only **5** to 10 percent of U.S. highways have speed limits of 65 **mph** or higher.

19. Many **whites** and Latinos attended the **Native American** culture festival.

20. The police seized a weapons cache that included five **.22-caliber** rifles and eight **9 mm** pistols.

21. Two of the biggest unions in the United States are the **United Auto Workers** and the United Steelworkers.

22. **African-Americans** constitute a plurality of the population in many U.S. cities.

23. The couple **were** married by the **imam**.

24. The majority of **Muslims** are Sunnis; **Shiites** are the largest minority sect. The holy book for both is the **Quran**.

HOMONYMS AND SOUND-ALIKES EXERCISE

a.	7	**k.**	35	**u.**	23	**ee.**	49	**oo.**	10
b.	31	**l.**	43	**v.**	9	**ff.**	30	**pp.**	12
c.	28	**m.**	45	**w.**	29	**gg.**	17	**qq.**	48
d.	22	**n.**	32	**x.**	33	**hh.**	15	**rr.**	36
e.	6	**o.**	16	**y.**	39	**ii.**	42	**ss.**	4
f.	19	**p.**	1	**z.**	44	**jj.**	40	**tt.**	25
g.	13	**q.**	5	**aa.**	21	**kk.**	20	**uu.**	8
h.	38	**r.**	34	**bb.**	11	**ll.**	2	**vv.**	27
i.	41	**s.**	18	**cc.**	14	**mm.**	46	**ww.**	3
j.	50	**t.**	26	**dd.**	47	**nn.**	37	**xx.**	24

COPY-EDITING SYMBOLS SELF-TEST

1. The expensive/leather briefcase was made in (N.J.) ⊗

   Delete comma because the adjectives *expensive* and *leather* are not coordinate. (*Not: The leather, expensive briefcase.*) Note the symbol: one line through the comma and an arc over the line. Circle *N.J.* to indicate that it should be spelled out. Insert a period to end the sentence.

2. The stunning long coat is made of 100 per cent cashmere.

   The adjectives *stunning* and *long* are coordinate (*the stunning, long coat; the long, stunning coat*), so a comma is necessary. Insert with a caret. *Percent*, according to AP, is one word. Use arcs top and bottom to close the space.

3. It has been a year's time since I hearrd "be good for goodness' sake."

   See AP under *possessives: quasi possessives, special expressions* for explanations on the need for apostrophes in *year's* and *goodness'*. Delete the extra *r* in *hearrd* with a line through the letter and arcs top and bottom.

4. I have an idea⊢⊣ you may not like it⊢⊣ that I think will work.

   The symbols for a dash (⊢⊣) and a hyphen (=) are different. Use dashes here for emphatic pauses.

5. Karim enrolled in the teachers° college.

   An apostrophe is unnecessary in *teachers* because it is descriptive, not possessive; see AP under *possessives*.

6. Mr. Jones is survived by his wife, Jana; a son, John, and a daughter, Joan.

   Use the semicolon before *and* in a complex series; insert with a caret.

7. Mr. Jones is survived by his wife, Jana, and a son, John.

   A comma to set off the nonessential *Jana* suffices here; two do not a series make.

8. The two-hour play was badly acted and ~~and~~ very dull.

   Hyphenate the compound adjective *two-hour*. Don't hyphenate "-ly" adverbs (AP: *-ly*). Use a top arc to bridge the space in deleting the redundant *and*.

9. The Pope will |Chicago| visit| next| week.

   Pope is not capitalized unless it precedes one or more names (AP: *titles*). Use the transpose symbol to invert words and letters.

10. The mass will be ~~said~~ (celebrated) at 11 a.m. (xxx day) in (Saint) Mark's Church.

    Mass is capitalized and is *celebrated*, not *said* (AP: *Mass*). Insert the missing day of the week according to AP's ordering of time-date-place. Indicate that *saint* should be abbreviated (AP: *saint*) by circling it.

11. The new ~~ambasader~~ will a^sume her duties on(October)15th.

    (ambassador)

    For clarity's sake, when a single word requires multiple corrections, strike it and rewrite; note original, incorrect spelling of *ambasader* requires two corrections. To add a single letter, as in *asume*, use a caret.

    Use a circle to indicate that *October* (like *January, February, August, September, November* and *December*) is abbreviated as part of a date — for which AP style requires cardinal numbers, not ordinal numbers (AP: *dates*).

    Using top and bottom arcs, close up the space between the numeral and the period at the end of the sentence.

12. "Take my advice and don't buy that car Jesse's father said.

    Put all three elements (the *r*, the comma and the end quote) in the "basket" for clarity.

13. The prescription for good health is threefold Proper diet, exercise and sufficient rest.

    Insert a colon to introduce the list and lowercase *proper* because it does not introduce an independent clause. Delete the comma after *exercise* to conform with AP style on serial commas.

14. "Can you give me a few [minutes]to get ready" Ellen asked.

    Use a caret to close the bracket around the inserted word in the quote; insert a question mark inside the quote mark because the quoted matter is a question.

PUNCTUATION/AP STYLE TEST

1. Chop some **wood,** or we won't be able to make a fire.

2. The president read his **statement** and left the briefing room without taking questions.

3. The meeting will be chaired by three **department heads:** Mark Sparks, **engineering;** Bill **Cash, finance;** and Faith **Morrow,** development.

4. The **congressional** delegation visited the disaster **site;** the governor stayed away.

5. Leslie had **homework,** but she didn't feel like doing it.

6. Lowell was the best designer on the **team** or he thought he was.

    or: ... **team** — **or** he thought ...

7. A good editor needs **three skills:** speed, **accuracy** and diplomacy.

8. Working through the bureaucracy is a **long,** tiresome process.

9. Marlo prefers **well-known brands,** which are usually more expensive.

   or: ... **brands that** are ...

10. Cigarette packages carry this warning (among others): "Cigarette Smoke Contains Carbon **Monoxide.**"

11. The CEO announced her **retirement** and then she took questions from reporters.

12. Reggie invited his oldest **sister, Rana,** and her **husband, Ralph,** to the party.

13. After **Hurricane Katrina** the **South** will never be the same.

14. I gave my grandmother's **necklace,** which is **100 years old,** to my **13-year-old** daughter.

15. Jimmy went on a diet, lost a lot of **weight** and bought new clothes.

GRAMMAR/AP STYLE TEST

1. The police considered **him** to be the primary suspect.

2. The jigsaw **puzzle,** which Ryan brought over **yesterday,** is still in the box.

   or: ... puzzle **that** Ryan brought over yesterday is ... *or:* delete *that*

3. The police asked **all the witnesses to** the accident for their phone numbers.

4. The Apollo 11 moon landing was **a** historic event.

5. The scout asked the coach **who** he thought was the most versatile player.

6. None of the economic experts surveyed **agrees** that a massive tax cut is good policy.

7. Peanut brittle is one of those sweets that **are** especially hard on the teeth.

8. The **committee** knew **whom** it would question first.

9. Makiko likes stock-car racing more **than she**.

10. I **laid** the reports on my desk yesterday but couldn't find **them** today.

11. The union submitted **its** list of demands.

12. Make sure that **whoever** you hire will fix the roof **quickly**.

13. If Danny **were** taller, he would try out for the basketball team.

14. I support **Ella** getting the award — she earned it!

15. Rupert **lay** awake until 3 a.m. worrying about his job interview.

16. This is the neighbor on **whom** I **depend** in emergencies.

17. Toronto is not **so** far from Chicago as Montreal.

18. I appreciate **your** watering my plants while I'm gone.

19. **Who** should I say is calling?

20. The defense mounted by Simpson's lawyers **was** unbeatable.

21. The crew boss hired **whoever** was available.

22. Romeo tells Juliet that neither the moon nor the stars **are so** brilliant as her eyes.

23. All **15** students know about the **quiz,** but none **is** studying for it.

24. For **whom** do you work?

25. There are no secrets between you and **me.**

26. Malika felt **bad** that she was the only one at the party **who** didn't bring a gift.

27. The **gas company** fired **its** chief **representative** after the power failure last summer.

28. Southwestern State has more recreational facilities than any **other** university in the area.

29. Stephen King is a writer **who** has had many of his novels made into films.

30. Jane Austen became my favorite author **after I read all of her novels.**

31. None of the economic experts **agree.**

32. The tollway bill that the governor proposed has no chance of passing. (**OK**)

   or: ... **bill, which** the governor **proposed,** has ...

33. We will **go either** to the Grand Canyon or to Yosemite.

34. **In 2000** the Bush-Gore presidential race **became** the first to be mediated by the Supreme Court.

USAGE/AP STYLE TEST

1. The exhibit **comprises/is composed of** 100 paintings.

2. I **expect** that the panel will **rebut** my theory when I defend my dissertation.

3. The judge said her **anti-abortion** views did not influence her ruling.

4. Over 200 **people living in the U.S. illegally** were killed by **drunken** drivers last year.

5. The three-member **committee comprises/is composed of** Jim, Jane and John.

6. Brian's uncle died **unexpectedly because of** a stroke, the doctor **said.**

7. The State **Department representative** would comment no **further.**

8. The Cubs' record did not **affect the** fans' loyalty.

9. Max is anxious about whether he will be able to **persuade** Judy to marry him.

10. You'll make **fewer** mistakes if you take a couple **of** minutes to review your answers.

11. Betsy's **experience** makes her the **No. 1** candidate for the position.

12. Lorelei was so **eager** to get the job that she was **champing** at the bit for the interview to begin.

13. When she called yesterday, Annie **implied** that she **hit/ran into** the parked car **because** she had been talking on her **cellphone** while driving.

14. Police said the victim had been **strangled**, but the coroner **declined to comment** before the autopsy was completed.

15. My father lost his **unique** pocket watch when a fire **destroyed** our house.

16. Rodrigo **said** it's not comfortable for him to compare his test score **with** his **roommate's**. *or:* ... **with that of** his roommate.

FINAL LANGUAGE-SKILLS TEST

1. Eddie **lay** awake with indigestion after eating pizza with hot peppers.

2. **Acme Inc.** is one of those companies that **have** increased the number of **their part-time** employees.

3. None of the negotiators agree. **(OK)**

4. Becky's project is as creative **as** or more creative **than** her **cousin's**.

5. The string quartet **comprises/is composed of** two violins, a viola and a harp.

6. Leila suggested **who** my choice for council president should be.

7. In his **email** Bob **implied** that he will apply for the position in Baltimore.

8. Nelligan was arrested on charges of strangling his **neighbor**.

9. **Who** would you say is the best woman for the job?

10. Between you and **me**, he knows more sports trivia **than I**.

11. My nephew's fashion sense is **unique**.

12. The **anti-abortion** activists wanted the school nurse fired because of her **pro-abortion-rights** stance.

13. The law students were **champing** at the bit for their bar-exam results.

14. When Marisol was **15,** she **immigrated** to the United States.

15. I appreciate **Judy's** editing my paper — that really made it better.

    or: I appreciate **Judy** editing my paper — **she** really made it better.

16. Mary's opinion about the death penalty is different **from** Tom's.

17. The museum's modern-art collection **comprises/is composed of/has** 30 paintings and 20 sculptures.

18. I asked Noni to buy a couple **of** extra bags of chips for the party.

19. "Your pleading will not **affect** the outcome," the judge said. "**It's** up to the jury to decide."

20. I wouldn't presume to compare my writing **to** Shakespeare's, but I would compare it with yours.

21. O'Donnell is the politician **whom** most Illinois voters admire.

22. When **the store** closed last month, **its** inventory was liquidated.

    or: When **it** closed last month, **the store** liquidated its inventory.

23. Undeterred by a string of recent setbacks that **includes** a car accident, Helen is meeting her deadlines in a way **that** her boss admires.

    or: ... **setbacks, which include** a car accident,
       ... setbacks **including** a car accident,

24. This is the kitten **that** climbed up the tree in my **backyard**.

25. The moving van **hit/crashed into** the garage.

26. The aroma of the grilling steaks **mingles** with the smell of roasted corn.

27. Jerome could edit faster than anyone **else** in his lab.

    or: Jerome **was the fastest editor** in his lab.

28. Harry's grandmother died **unexpectedly**.

29. Angie feels **bad** that she wasn't invited.

30. Reggie **laid** his keys on the table an hour **ago,** but now he cannot find **them**.

31. The Red Sox manager congratulated everyone for playing **his** best.

32. If Bashar **were** taking **fewer classes,** he would volunteer more.

33. Michael Jordan is one of those athletes who have carved **places** for **themselves** in sports history.

34. None of these dresses **is** appropriate to wear to the wedding.

35. The **paper,** which I worked on all **night,** is due tomorrow.

    or: The paper **that** I worked on all night is due tomorrow. *or:* delete *that*

36. **Hopefully,** I'll be able to take a break soon.

37. The explosion **destroyed** the building.

38. The nanny told the boy to **lie** down.

39. Over 2 million people in the U.S., **Europe** and Asia protested the war.

40. All of the **Writers** Guild members went on strike, but none was sure the union would win.

41. The editor **said,** "There are three things I cannot **stand: misspellings,** sloppy **punctuation** and buried leads."

42. Disaster was **averted because of** Meredith's quick thinking.

43. Roxanne is as talented as **Jennifer** but not **so well-known** as **she**.

44. Neither french fries nor potato chips **are** permitted on your diet.

45. The doctors **expected** that Henry's recovery would be difficult.

46. I was **persuaded** to vote for Yamamoto after he convinced me that he was right on the issues.

47. The candidate **declined to** comment on her opponent's marital **problems** and she quickly changed the subject.

48. The firm is considering changing **its** location.

49. After the **five-hour** meeting, Sanjay was **eager** to eat lunch.

50. None of the parties **agrees** to the proposal.

51. **Second-** and **third-rate** films won't make the cut at the Chicago Film Festival.

52. The defense **refuted** the prosecution's argument, and the defendant was acquitted.

53. Here's a better **idea:** I'll order the **pizza,** and you pick it up.

54. Errol lost his wallet, **and that** made him angry.

    or: Errol lost his wallet, **making** him angry.

    Errol was angry because he lost his wallet.

55. Bonnie asked **who** I thought the graduation speaker would be.

FACT-CHECKING EXERCISE

1. In his speech, Howe stressed the significance of religion in American thought in the 19th century. He noted that when the **trans-Atlantic** cable was first laid in **1858**, Queen Victoria and President **Buchanan** exchanged the first message with a **biblical** quotation.

2. A little boy collapses on a wide wooden bench.

   "Don't you want to see the **Seurat**?" his mother asks.

   "I want to sit down," he says.

   Shaking her head, she turns to ponder the painting. Some stare at the work through the lenses of their phones, the magnitude of "A Sunday Afternoon on the **Island** of **La** Grande **Jatte**" captured on a screen no bigger than the palm of a hand.

3. The city of Oakville employee daycare budget will increase **5.4** percent next fiscal year, Mayor Emily Harakawa announced on Monday. Effective July 1, the budget will increase by **$633** to $12,270 from $11,637, she said.

4. In July 2013 Illinois became the last state in the U.S. to **pass** a **concealed** carry act, after a federal appeals court ruled it unconstitutional for the state to continue its ban on concealed weapons. This act legally enables citizens to carry some types of concealed weapons, heightening concerns of proponents for **tighter** gun restrictions.

5. SEOUL, **South** Korea — The rival Koreas agreed Wednesday to hold their first reunions of Korean War-divided families in more than three years later this month, another small step to ease tensions despite North Korea's anger over upcoming U.S.-South **Korean** military drills.

TIGHTENING EXERCISE

1. Attorney and activist Rondi Vega will deliver this year's women's leadership lecture at Southeastern University on March 27.

2. Many U.S. college students have expressed support for President Obama's views on marijuana use published in The New Yorker this week.

3. Grantham discussed how ideas are spread through social networks.

4. As hundreds of incoming Arcadia students gathered on Greening Meadow on a mid-September day at sunset, one freshman stood tall above the rest.

5. Commuters are finding it impossible to escape the extreme cold pounding the Midwest — not even the "Frostbite Express" shuttle provides relief.

6. A man was found dead Wednesday night in Fernwood after a shooting in Oakdale, and police have no leads.

CLARITY EXERCISE

(P1) From what percentage to what percentage (starting and ending points) were the 1.3 percent and 1.1 percent drops over the past year?

(P2) What other types of jobs is Marks qualified for and interested in?

(P3) Is Washington employed, and if so, what is his job? What degree did he earn?

(P4) What is Dodd studying, and what employment related to customer service will she seek after college?

(P5) What is Clark studying, and what kind of "prestigious professional job" does he hope for after graduation?

QUOTATIONS AND ATTRIBUTION EXERCISE

1. Jesse Brown has been a newspaper editor for 30 years but **says** technology has not changed many of the basics.

   "Journalists still have to exercise news judgment, cultivate sources and use language clearly**," he said.** "**Most important, they** need to be ethical in their reporting methods and balanced in their **presentation.**

   "These common denominators **don't** change, no matter what new technologies enable us to do," **Brown said.**

2. "I started researching my family history 15 years ago," **said** Jane Findlay**, 85.** "**I knew about** nothing before my grandparents' generation. **The more** I found out, the more fascinating it became.**"

   Findlay said **keeping her family history alive is important and that she will continue researching as long as she can.** "This is my gift to my grandchildren and to their children one day," **she said.**

3. Gov.-elect Royce Brauner said on Tuesday that he will **not "do business as usual" and vowed to cut costly programs and change labor practices.**

   "I will **effect** change in every way I know how," **he** said, including **new approaches to attracting business investment.**

Index

About the Author

Marda Dunsky has been a professional editor and teacher of editing for over 30 years. She teaches at the Medill School of Journalism, Media, Integrated Marketing Communications at Northwestern University.

Dunsky worked as a features and national/foreign news editor at the *Chicago Tribune*. She also has worked as a copy editor at the *Sun-Sentinel* in Fort Lauderdale, Florida, and the *Telegram & Gazette* in Worcester, Massachusetts.

Dunsky has served as an editorial consultant to the *Chicago Tribune*, where she trained more than 400 editors and reporters in editing and language-skills seminars. She also has conducted editing seminars and presentations for Tribune Media Services, Tribune Interactive and the Media Management Center at Northwestern University.

Other editorial consulting clients have included UNICEF, the Inland Press Foundation, *The Arizona Republic*, *The Indianapolis Star*, Hill & Knowlton and Kalmbach Publishing.

Dunsky is also the author of *Pens and Swords: How the American Mainstream Media Report the Israeli-Palestinian Conflict* (Columbia University Press, 2008).

CPSIA information can be obtained at www.ICGtesting.com
Printed in the USA
BVOW09s1714200615

405277BV00001B/1/P

9 781442 253438